Rebuilding the Tower of Babel

the Dark Side of the Purpose-Driven, New Paradigm Church

MAC DOMINICK

CUTTING EDGE MINISTRIES
www.cuttingedge.org

Rebuilding the Tower of Babel: The Dark Side of the Purpose-Driven, New Paradigm Church

For more information on Cutting Edge Ministries, please visit our website at www.cuttingedge.org.

All Scripture quotations taken from the Authorized King James Version.

ISBN:0-9768167-1-7

Rebuilding the Tower of Babel:
The Dark Side of the Purpose-Driven, New Paradigm Church

TABLE OF CONTENTS

FORWARD

My brother in Christ, Mac Dominick, has written this his second book on the evil and fallout from the advent of the Outcome-based, seeker friendly church mentality; and now he addresses Rick Warren in particular! Mac is as a follower of the actual Jesus of Nazareth. The absolutely holy and righteous Christ that Paul the Apostle preached--not the sin inclusive, politically correct christ (small "c" intentional) that has been recently substituted by the Rick Warrens of the world.

I first met Mac Dominick three years ago at a seminar put on by Cutting Edge Ministries based on Mac's first book, *Outcome Based Religion*. Sadly, I arrived late as the lecture was wrapping up, but I was amazed to see a couple hundred people there. I introduced myself and talked with Mac briefly.

I purchased the DVD version of the seminar to see what my friends were going on about. I was blown away while watching as Mac in the video proceeded giving the history of the modern Evangelical Church. My Church, a large Southern Baptist Church in Atlanta, Georgia had just done the *Purpose Driven Life* program, and I had become concerned with the liberties and slack attitude Dr. Warren exhibited toward the *Bible*.

Three years later I got in touch with the people at Cutting Edge to see if I might contact Mr. Dominick. I had a question concerning a quote Dr. Warren used making the Tower of Babel a positive example of what mankind could do if they worked together. I was even more concerned when I noticed it was delivered on the High Holy Day for Satanists--Halloween. I eventually heard back from Mac and we talked about Dr. Warren and how rapidly things progressed since I first met him.

As a result of this conversation, Mac offered to give a mini lecture to people at my Church concerned with Warren's new *40 Days of P.E.A.C.E.* program which was on the church's docket. A deacon and other influential people at my Church were there. The attendee's were blown away as I had been years earlier.

As of the time of this writing, I and a couple of other brothers from my church have been compiling a report intended for the elders and pastor of the church. I have spent 8 months researching Rick Warren and his Saddleback mega-Church Empire to get an overview of the true gist of his message.

I woke up early one morning to write an introductory paragraph on the message section of our report on Dr. Warren. As I began to ponder the things Dr. Warren said about his purpose and his plan, I realized the similarities between Dr. Warren and a notorious character from 20th century history. I noted the similarities, thinking that it was an interesting aside, but a little over the top. I always disliked these type of analogies because they are too often inappropriately used or just "grasping at straws" to prove a point.

As I worked on the paper several hours later, I heard the familiar sound of Rick Warren's voice on TV. As he uttered these words the hairs on the back of my neck stood up as a chill ran through my body:

> "I look at this stadium and I think about how in the late 1930's, 100,000 young people in brown shirts packed into the Olympic stadium in Germany, and they formed with their bodies a sign for a fanatical man standing behind a podium a man with a mustache --Adolph Hitler. And the sign said, *we are yours*. And they nearly took the world." (1)

Rick Warren's message is a simple one! He wants to change the world. He has a *Plan*: Dr. Warren proclaimed in Angel's Stadium full of his cheering followers that his purpose for being alive is to implement the *Global P.E.A.C.E. Plan.* We will remind you that Adolph Hitler, standing in front of a stadium full of his followers said the same thing.

Warren is convinced that his plan is *God's dream*. How does he interpret this dream? Just as he parroted a statement by his mentor, Peter Drucker:

> "'I once heard Drucker say this,' Warren said. Warren is not building a tent revival ministry, like the old-style evangelists. He's building an army, like the Jesuits.'" (2)

Dr. Warren's *Global P.E.A.C.E. Plan* is perched atop a political, economic and religious *three legged stool*--the very same socio-economic, theocratic stool upon which Hitler built his plan of global dominion. Hitler claimed to be a Christian, but he didn't gather those 100,000 plus followers to pray and fast at Nuremburg did he? No, they were giving praise and allegiance to a man. When Rick Warren gets a Stadium full of people to swear to God to follow through with a plan that was not instituted by God, is he not doing the same thing?

This new book by Mac Dominick will prove Rick Warren's plan is not God's plan by its fruit and from God's own Holy Word. Thus, if it is not God's plan, whose plan is it? Hmmm???? Let us ponder this for a minute. Who wants to bring the world together as one? Who wants to appear to solve all the world's problems, replacing Jesus of Nazareth with?????

Dr. Warren has cobbled together his plan with the help of a rainbow coalition of management gurus, heretics, occultists and of misguided but well meaning Christians. This plan has been concocted by taking elements of biblical teachings, management theory, psychology, pseudo science, occult practices—and cooked them into a global apostasy stew that the world is gobbling up. To his credit, Dr. Warren has indeed figured out how to fill many a church-- but not with truly born-again saints. His accomplishments have been very impressive in a Tower of Babel sort of way.

He can fix your church with a few minor adjustments. Get rid of that name Baptist Church! Take down that cross. Rip out those pews. Take out the stained glass, and that organ just has to go!!!! If you prefer holding fast to the *Bible*, you're expendable in his new church. Those hymns, that choir-- forget it.

According to Dr. Warren, God really prefers *Rock and Roll* rather than hymns. Dr. Warren has assured us that "*All music is God's music*," and of course, Dr. Warren's words are authoritative because he has been given his vision by God. How else would he sell 30,000,000 books if God weren't behind him, right? I guess you should tell that to Ozzy Ozbourne or Led Zeppelin. They sold many millions more albums and compact discs than Dr. Warren has books. Last time I checked, they weren't wearing halos or angel's wings-- were they? So who helped Ozzy and Zeppelin? No it wasn't Gabriel. It was, however, another angel. An angel who got his pink slip a long time ago!

Dr. Warren's message dictates that if traditional churches aren't growing, the pastors and churches need another way of *doing church*, and they are in sin if they do not change their methods. By the way, it was Dr. Warren and his accomplices that began using the expression *doing church*. People *do drugs*! To the contrary, Christians do not *do church*. Christians gather together in the name of the Lord for worship, edification, and fellowship, but *doing church* is a foreign concept that borders on insolence, insubordination, and blasphemy.

Unfortunately for Dr. Warren, this is a lie from the pit of Hell. Jesus Christ expects his Church and his people to be faithful, to preach the Word in season and out of season, to share the Gospel—the good news of the death, burial, and resurrection for the redemption of lost mankind. This is the essence of the true Gospel that teaches mankind is desperately wicked, in bondage to sin, and needs to fall at the foot of the cross and repent. It is only the perfect and innocent blood of Christ that cleanses fallen man and makes a relationship with God even possible.

I thank God for Mac Dominick, for Cutting Edge Ministries, and the faithful men and women of God out there like them who are the believers standing for the Truth of Jesus Christ. The time is coming and is already at hand when Truth will be very hard to find on this earth.

All must remember that Truth has a name--- and that name is Jesus.

Your Servant in Christ
Robert L. LeBus

(1) Warren, Rick. Excerpt from a speech at the Hillsong Conference in Australia, 2006.
(2) Gladwell, Malcolm. The Cellular Church, New Yorker Magazine, 09.12.05.

Rebuilding the Tower of Babel:

The Dark Side of the Purpose-Driven, New Paradigm Church

By
Mac Dominick

Introduction

This is not a fairy tale, nor is it a sweet bedtime story. This is a warning of the gravest kind. It is a warning of evil, and on a day forty-three hundred years ago evil had a name that by its very definition of "let us rebel" personified the diabolical character of Lucifer's servant, Nimrod.

The Bible calls Nimrod a "mighty hunter before the Lord," but the ancient Hebrew rabbis interpreted this as meaning he was a hunter of men's souls. In support of the rabbinical interpretation, many Bible scholars insist that the original Hebrew language of the book of Genesis would be better understood if translated "a mighty hunter *against* the Lord," signifying a rebellion against God unparalleled in the entire postdiluvian civilization.

On this particular day so long ago, the Great Hunter stood in awe as the sun fractured the eastern horizon of the Plain of Shinar and ignited the predawn sky into a myriad of color. The shimmering rays of light that exploded from the sky and danced across the colossal structure gave him a profound sense of pride and great accomplishment as few have ever felt. The instructions had been explicit, the plans had been executed perfectly to the minutest detail, and now the magnificent tower that would serve as catalyst to the culture and technology of the not-too-distant past was becoming a reality.

He stood as the Mighty Colossus of Rhoades atop the magnificent structure. Looking down on the mass of humanity assembled far below his feet gave him a godlike feeling; and to his subjects, he held the godlike position of holding in his hands the power of life and death.

Now the Great Hunter was on the very precipice of proving that a united, motivated, human race could accomplish anything—even if such an accomplishment was diametrically opposed to the plan of God. With these intoxicating thoughts flowing through his consciousness, Nimrod basked in the warmth of the sun and the pure euphoria of personal achievement. However, this very day God Himself would not only thwart his ambitious plans of a world empire, but also deny the immanent appearance of a single universal religion that would accompany any such political aspirations.

The construction would stop, and the lofty dreams of Nimrod would be shattered. But even with his subsequent death and dismemberment (Jewish scholars teach that Nimrod was executed by Noah's righteous son, Shem, his body cut into 14 pieces, and the pieces subsequently distributed to his followers as an acute warning of rebellion.), (1) the esoteric religion would live on. With the help of Nimrod's widow Semiramis and her illegitimate son Tammuz, the Ancient Wisdom would be carefully preserved in the Babylonian Mystery Religions. (2) As the followers of Nimrod scattered across the face of the earth, the Ancient Mysteries accompanied them from Egypt, to China, and to even to the Americas. With the passing of time, the Ancient Wisdom came to be guarded by the "elite wise persons" of Babylon, Medo-Persia, Pergamos, and Rome. It later found a home in Eastern Religions, the Jewish Kabbalah, and Western Gnosticism. (3)

THE LEGACY OF THE TOWER OF BABEL

After the turn of the Third Century AD, the power of the Church of Rome began to rise, and this directly developed into a schism among the keepers of the Mysteries. When Constantine moved to legalize Christianity, the Roman Church embraced many of the doctrines of the Babylonian Mystery Religions. As a result, the Church of Rome adopted the worship of the mother and child, infant baptism, confession to a priest, and many other practices of the Babylonian Mysteries. The Church did not embrace the occult aspects of the Mystery Religions, but these remained with the Mystery Schools of the East, Kabbalists, and Gnostics until the time of the crusades. However, the purely occult side of the Ancient Wisdom surfaced publicly in Western Europe with the rise of the Merovingian Dynasty and the legends of "Parcival and the

Quest for the Holy Grail." The subsequent schism within the "mystery schools" of "white and black magick" exploded into a major conflict when the Knights Templar (The Order of the Temple) returned from the crusades as the wealthiest men on earth.

The Knights Templar and secret societies like the Prieure' de Sion (The Order of Zion) became the cultural elite that fully embraced the dark, most occult aspects of the Ancient Mysteries. This put them on a collision course with the Church of Rome and her allies. The Prieure' de Sion went underground and disappeared from the pages of history (until revived in the 1950s by Pierre Plantard), while the members of the Knights Templar were viciously attacked by Catholic puppet, King Philippe IV of France, and Pope Clement V.

On October 13th, 1307, Philippe ordered the arrest of all Knights Templar. However, the prior evening, an unknown number of Knights Templar sailed from France with a reported eighteen galleys loaded with the legendary Templar Treasure. (4) At least a portion of the Templars sailed to Scotland, and organizing with the Scots Guard, Rosicrucians, Invisible College, and Royal Society (all occult groups) formed the Scottish Rite of Freemasonry. (5) The Freemasons appropriated the Templars as antecedents, as well as authorizing custody of their arcane secrets. (6) As a result, the Scottish Rite is "magically oriented, emphasizes a sacred social and political hierarchy, a divine order, and an underlying cosmic plan." (7) This is the very essence of the Ancient Mysteries of Nimrod.

From this sequence of historical events, one who is acquainted with the Word of God, and particularly Bible prophecy, can logically conclude the following:

1) Nimrod sought to restore the pre-flood system of a world government, led by a priest-king, and empowered directly by Lucifer.
2) When God spoiled Nimrod's plan, Lucifer's strategy was altered to set up a system of false religions that would hold in store these powerful Ancient Mysteries until the time that he (Lucifer) could succeed in establishing such a kingdom.

3) These Mysteries have been guarded since that time by a select, elite group. There have been periods of history that publicly accepted the darker (occult) side of the mysteries and periods when the occult has been suppressed.
4) The Bible records that a future world kingdom will arise led by the Beast (Antichrist), who will declare himself as the Christ. This world kingdom will be accompanied by a one-world church until such time that it is no more useful to the Beast. The Beast will also declare himself to be the Messiah of the Jews and rightful heir to the throne of David.
5) The Beast will reveal the secrets of the Ancient Mysteries that have been so faithfully guarded by his servants for millennia as proof of his position to fully establish his kingdom.

The process of the inevitable demise of modern society that will culminate at Armageddon began with Nimrod and the construction of the Tower of Babel. The Ancient Mystery Religions were in direct opposition to the worship the God of the Bible, Nimrod was the servant of Lucifer, and the Tower of Babel was the catalyst of defiance against the plan of God for the human race. As a result of these facts, even the vaguest reference to the Tower of Babel as a positive image for any honorable undertaking was absolutely unthinkable for the four millennia since construction was abandoned.

This perception began to change in the 1980s when the image of the Tower of Babel began to appear on promotional material for the European Union. This, of course, should come as no surprise to the biblically astute individual who understands the total ramifications of modern political globalism. For the EU is, if nothing else, the embodiment of the Luciferian philosophies that will pave the road to Armageddon.

RICK WARREN'S 40 DAYS OF COMMUNITY

However, there are very recent positive references to the Tower of Babel that can be put in no other terms than "completely inexplicable." Furthermore, these references did not originate from a Luciferian, globalistic secular source, but from the pulpit of a "conservative" Baptist church. Without doubt, many sermons have been preached from the pulpits of Bible-believing churches that that have characterized the Tower of Babel as an example of rebellion against God and the object of His judgment. However, on October 30-31, 2004, the pulpit of Saddleback Community Church (Southern Baptist Convention) in south Orange County, California, was in all likelihood the first ecclesiastical location in history from which the Tower of Babel would be presented as an example of what individual members of the Church could accomplish when functioning in concert. In addition, many of the 700 churches chosen to pilot *40 Days of Community* at the same time may have used this positive promotion of the Tower of Babel (This author has received notification of at least one other church that witnessed this very illustration).

The pastor of Saddleback Community Church, Dr. Rick Warren, was in the midst of his latest 40-day campaign, *40 Days of Community*. The *40 Days of Community* program is a 6-week emphasis on building "community" within the Church, and Dr. Warren's example of the Tower of Babel was given at the conclusion of the 4th week. In essence, Dr. Warren related that the Tower of Babel was a perfect example of what could be accomplished when men and women work together to reach a common goal. He stated that the construction crew of the Tower of Babel worked so well as a group that God had to intervene to separate them.

The context of this characterization and comparison of the events that occurred on the Plain of Shinar so long ago with that which can be accomplished by the members of the "Body of Christ" unified by the bond of the Holy Spirit should make the blood of a true child of God run ice cold. How could Dr. Warren violate the context of Scripture to the extreme that would result in such a comparison? Does he have no concept of Evil as personified by Nimrod? Does he not realize the rebellious source of empowerment of those who built the tower? Does he not understand the historical and prophetic significance that stems from the events at Babel? Does he discount the power of the Holy Spirit working within the child of God in order to accomplish God's purposes? Does he dismiss the Scripture that states that God's strength is made perfect in man's weakness? Why would a minister of the Gospel of Jesus Christ glorify one of the most renowned examples of rebellion against God in all of history? Is this a warning of deeper issues with the *40 Days of Community* program? Could this illustration possibly be a signal to undisclosed observers that there is more to *40 Days of Community* than meets the eye?

OCCULT GLORIFICATION OF THE GROUP

The basic concepts of Warren's *40 Days of Community* are all based upon the formation and functioning of small groups within the church and the theme that "we are better together." While there is no doubt that the Word of God teaches unity among believers, the concepts and terminology used in the *40 Days of Community* campaign raises many red warning flags. However, these "red flags" become more like screaming sirens when one realizes the permeation of the "group-think" mentality held by occult, pagan, and earth-based religions that originated at the Tower of Babel.

The Jewish historian, Flavius Josephus, wrote of the Tower of Babel from a unique perspective. Josephus stated that after the Flood, God commanded mankind to disperse across the face of the earth and populate the entire globe. In lieu of following the commands of God, mankind followed the leadership of Nimrod. Nimrod and his followers realized that they were in direct defiance to the commandments of God, and they chose to build a tower that would "reach to heaven" to provide a way to escape the wrath of God in the event of another flood. They all worked together to insure the survival of the species. They functioned as a group in order to preserve the group. (8)

Once these men were dispersed across the face of the planet, this "group-think" philosophy then permeated occult thought from this point in history forward. It has been seen throughout history and in modern occult, "new-age," and neo-pagan thought. Group-think philosophies are readily perceptible in modern theosophical writings, earth-based nature religions, eastern religion, goddess worship, Luciferian organizations, outcome-based education, and now (thanks to Dr. Warren) the "Evangelical Church."

LUCERFERIAN PHILOSOPHIES IN THE CHURCH

Unfortunately, many Christians are duped into following a Luciferian agenda because they have no real concept of the beliefs and methods of occult and esoteric religions, and are so detached from the leading of God's Holy Spirit that they have no sense whatsoever of discernment of that which is truly good and that which is truly evil. In other words, this generation of evangelicals is ripe for deception. The deceptive agenda is cleverly disguised as a "new way of doing church," "building community" among the body of believers, and a host of other systems and programs.

The average Christian (whether conservative, evangelical, or fundamentalist) has very little knowledge of the true workings of the occult world. This, of course, is not surprising, for those who "name the name of Jesus Christ" naturally, and as a matter of course, avoid religious discussions with those who would participate in occult practices. Not only that, but the workings of the "forces of darkness" are generally perceived as evil, macabre rituals that are too terrifying for the average individual (Christian or not) to comprehend, much less cerebrally reconcile on any logical level. Furthermore, the perception of an individual involved in occult practices is one of placing that individual on a lunatic fringe of society. However, not only are these perceptions grossly inaccurate, but there exists a distinct, lurking danger associated with this lack of knowledge—for if Evil were always readily identifiable as Evil—very few would be enticed into its clutches. Therefore, the strategy of Lucifer is not always that of the grotesque or macabre; but as the Word of God warns, he appears as an "angel of light."

It is within this context that one must evaluate the recent events within Evangelical and Fundamentalist Christianity. For the latest movements in the construction of the purpose-driven, outcome-based, New Paradigm Church share some very eerie and very disconcerting similarities to the dark forces of the occult, and it is these very similarities this manuscript will seek to address. In essence, it will further examine these occult concepts and establish how modern evangelicals who claim to be "building the Kingdom of God" are, in reality, *Rebuilding the Tower of Babel.*

END NOTES

(1) Hislop, Alexander. *The Two Babylons*, Loizeaux Bros.Pub., 1916, p.56.

(2) Ibid. p.20.

(3) Kah, Gary. *En Route to Global Occupation*, Huntington House, 1991, p. 94.

(4) Baigent & Leigh. *The Temple and the Lodge*, Arcade Pub., 1989, p. 53.

(5) Ibid. p. 155.

(6) Baigent, Lincoln & Leigh. *Holy Blood, Holy Grail,* Dell Pub., 1982, p. 65.

(7) Ibid. p. 197.

(8) Flavius Josephus. *The Antiquities of the Jews*, Book I, Chapter IV.

Chapter 1

The Angel of Light

The members of every past generation embraced the notion that their time was the pivotal point in human history, and to varying degrees, each one has been correct in this assessment. This concept applies not only to secular society and humanity in general, but also to specific segments of the world's population; and the present world population is no exception to this mentality. In the context of this manuscript, the world's occult and Christian populations are both acutely cognizant of the fact of humanity's position poised at the climax of the current "age" and are endowed with a distinct sense of revolutionary, imminent change.

As a prime example, in a 1989 speech to the Association of Supervision and Curriculum Development, Dr. Jean Houston dogmatically stated that this very generation will determine whether the human race will grow to a new, heightened level of consciousness or annihilate itself:

> "All cultures thought their culture was 'it.' They were wrong, this is 'it'—this time in history...the great 'time of either/or'...Everything is in place to make the leap, the jump phenomenon...We are living the passion of the loaded time...Grow or die...when what you and I do will profoundly make a difference." (1)

Dr. Houston went on to speak of a "whole system transition to a planetary society." Her definition of a planetary society is quite simple: a planetary society is based on an interdependent, centralized social democracy that encompasses an entire human race whose collective consciousness will expand to the point that each individual realizes that he or she is, in fact, "god." This very mindset and mantra spans the course of paganism, Wicca, New Age, and other earth-based religions that comprise a major segment of what is deemed the "occult world."

On the other end of the spectrum, the members of the Church are convinced that this indeed is, a critical, pivotal moment in human history.

Those who are Dispensational in their theology and hold to a literal interpretation of Scripture believe that the "end of the age" that will culminate with the Rapture of the Church, the Kingdom of Antichrist, and the subsequent Second Coming is very close. In addition, the events seen as the obvious fulfillment of Bible Prophecy that began in 1948 with the establishment of Israel as a nation continue to occur.

THE CHURCH OF THE NEW PARADIGM

Imbedded into the dispensational theological framework is also the realization that the Church of Jesus Christ is facing a major shift away from the "Old Time Religion" of its fathers and grandfathers. This shift is not a minor adjustment, but rather, a major change that threatens to alter the face of Christianity forever. Tragically, if this shift continues unchecked, the subsequent change will create a new "hybrid Christianity" that will bear little resemblance to the "faith of our fathers" or the Church as described in the New Testament. This new hybrid is instead birthing a "false Christianity" that will lead its adherents to a pseudo-faith that will result in their missing the Rapture, believing "a lie," (2) and falling into the arms of Antichrist as gently as the falling petals of an autumn rose.

This new hybrid Christianity was described first by Rick Warren in his book, *The Purpose-Driven Church* as a "paradigm shift" or a new way of thinking about Christianity. The terminology of a "new paradigm" or a "paradigm shift" was derived from Thomas Kuhn, who coined the term "paradigm" in 1973. The term was then popularized by Marilyn Ferguson in her book, *The Aquarian Conspiracy* that is described as "the New Age Bible." The use of "new age" terminology is even more distressing when one understands the introduction of a "third way" philosophy of the radical center. The "third way" is a deceptive radical philosophy cloaked in the skin of conservative or fundamental pretenses. Thus, the Church of the New Paradigm represents a shift in how one thinks about the church---or how one "does church." It is a church that is outwardly conservative or even fundamental, but whose essence is entirely radical.

John MacArthur very astutely described this shift in his book, *Reckless Faith* when he stated:

- There has been a shift in Evangelical consensus
- This shift is short on doctrine and long on experience
- Thinking is deemed less important than feeling
- Love of sound doctrine has disappeared
- Add a dose of mysticism and you have the recipe for unmitigated spiritual disaster. (3)

The shift MacArthur describes is the exact course traversed by those involved in what has come to be popularly termed the "Church Growth Movement" (CGM). The methodology of this movement among Christian Evangelicals and Fundamentalists materialized in the second half of the Twentieth Century and was championed by Fuller Theological Seminary. The manifestation of the movement is now seen in the seeker-sensitive mega-churches mushrooming into existence all over the nation.

The "poster child" of the Church Growth Movement, Dr. Rick Warren of Saddleback Community Church, has proclaimed that the church is in the midst of a culture-changing revolution, (4) and those involved in his specific programs are the revolutionary leaders that will initiate the "paradigm shift" that will swell throughout all of Christendom. However, upon close examination of these programs---"40 Days of Purpose," "40 Days of Community," and "40 Days of P.E.A.C.E."—as well as Dr. Warren's books—*The Purpose-Driven Church* and *The Purpose-Driven Life*-- not only does one start to question their doctrinal position-- but also the subtle introduction of occult philosophies and terminologies into an arena that outwardly touts the fulfillment of "The Great Commission" as its sole outcome.

In order to thoroughly assess this entire situation, an understanding must be reached on the Luciferian methodologies and teachings of the occult world. Once such an understanding is achieved, then a fair appraisal can be made of the programs that drive the Church Growth Movement --alias the Church of the New Paradigm.

IN THE BEGINNING

Lucifer's first appearance in the Word of God is found in the account of the temptation of Eve in the Garden of Eden. Due to the familiarity of the text, many read this passage without giving much thought to all of the ramifications associated with the actual sequence of events of that eternally fateful day. However, when one considers the details of the conversation recorded in Scripture and its results, a few conclusions become quite obvious:

- If the theories of evolution were actually true, Eve would never have bought into the lie, "Ye shalt not surely die." The obvious reason for this conclusion is the simple fact that Eve, to this point in her life, never witnessed anyone or anything die. Even in the case of "Theistic Evolution," Eve would have witnessed death as a natural course of life. However, since the biblical facts reveal that Evolution (Theistic or otherwise) is false, Eve herself had been created but a relatively short time in an environment that was not yet under the curse of sin. Therefore, in her innocent state, she never witnessed death of any kind, she never planned to die; and subsequently, Eve believed the lies of Lucifer when he contradicted the consequences of disobedience as outlined by God.

- Lucifer only succeeded in deceptively luring Eve by making the Tree of Knowledge of Good and Evil and its forbidden fruit appear as something to be desired. He played the ultimate game of deception—transforming the very object that would lead Eve to her death to deceptively appear as something enticingly and irresistibly desirable.

- Lucifer also appealed to Eve's ego by offering the elevation of her status to that of a "god" when he stated, "thou shall be as gods." Eve only knew one God, God the Ruler and Creator of all things. To be as God, rule as God, and know what God knew was the "golden carrot" that lured Eve into sin.

Once these conclusions are considered, further reflection on these very aspects of the conversation that transpired in the Garden of Eden so many years ago reveals the very foundation of Luciferian thought as the antithesis to the Word of God. That foundation rests upon three cornerstones:

- Acceptance of the theory of Evolution as a fact
- A strategy of deception that promotes evil as good.
- A philosophy of monistic pantheism

EVOLUTION AND OCCULT THOUGHT

Very few people are aware of the events that led to the presentation of Charles Darwin's theories on origins to Great Britain's 19th Century scientific community. Darwin was aided in his research by his very close friend, Charles Lyell. Lyell stood by the reluctant Darwin for more than twenty years of painstaking research in the development of his theories. Additionally, Darwin was not a seeker of fame and notoriety. As a matter of fact, he was very hesitant to bring his work into the public forum of the intellectual community. (5)

However, the day arrived that Darwin was forced to publicly present his theories or else not only be upstaged by another, but witness the loss of all of his efforts. In 1855, Darwin received a copy of a paper written by Alfred Russell Wallace that detailed the same theories that he himself painstakingly developed over the course of 20 years. Darwin then immediately, at Lyell's urging, began writing his infamous work, *The Origin of Species*. Both Darwin and Wallace, however, were seeking the missing key component—the mechanism by which one species could effectively change into another. (The problem with the absence of such a mechanism is obvious, for there is absolutely no evidence [scientific or otherwise] that provides one shred of proof that one species has, or ever will evolve into another species.)

Three years after sending his paper on origins to Darwin, Wallace became very ill while living on the island of Ternate. In the violent throes of a debilitating fever, a vision of the missing mechanism came to him in a "moment's revelation." Wallace then sent that mechanism, *The Survival of the Fittest*, to Darwin. The *Ternate Paper* contained "in complete form, what is today known as the Darwinian Theory of Evolution..." (6) In reality, the circumstantial evidence strongly suggests that Darwin plagiarized many of the key concepts of the infamous *Origin of Species* from Wallace's work. However, since Wallace was closer to New Guinea than to London when the presentation time arrived, the concepts presented to the Linnean Society in July of 1858 became known as the Darwin/Wallace Theory.

That, of course, is not the entire story. Alfred Russell Wallace not only received the "vision" of *The Survival of the Fittest* to complete the evolutionary lie of Lucifer while delirious with fever, but Wallace harbored a much darker side. During his early life, Wallace traveled to the Amazon and befriended Indians who shared with him their "black arts." Wallace then began to dabble in Spiritism, and he was openly ridiculed for his membership in the Society for Psychical Research. The extreme level that he became involved in the occult resulted in his virtual expulsion from Britain's intellectual community, not to mention the removal of his name from the Darwinian theories.

In the case of his *Ternate Paper*, the method of scientific discovery utilized by Wallace went beyond the unorthodox into the realm of the metaphysical. As a matter of fact, revelations such as his are not uncommon in the realm of the "occult sciences," and from a biblical perspective, this experience can be accurately placed into the category of demonic communication methodology. (The Koran was communicated to the illiterate Mohammed in the midst of similar convulsions.)

The point here, however, is a specific demonic connection to the public presentation and proliferation of evolutionary theories into mainstream society. Additionally, few realize that the men of the 19th Century who shaped the evolutionary and socialistic philosophies destined to permeate the future of mainstream society had little in common, and most were not formally educated as scientists. Charles Darwin had a degree in theology, Charles Lyell was a lawyer, Thomas Huxley had a dubious degree in medicine, Jean-Baptiste Lamarck and Herbert Spencer had no formal education, and Hegel and Marx had degrees in philosophy. There was, however, one thing that each of these men shared—a hatred of God and biblical Christianity. (7)

Based on all of the above, there should be no surprise in learning that occult philosophies and pagan religions operate from a baseline of evolutionary thought. These evolutionary principles within the occult world are actually based on another lie that Lucifer told Eve in the Garden of Eden: "Ye shalt be as gods..." New Agers, witches, and adherents to other earth-based religions believe that man is divine and simply needs to discover or develop the god or goddess within. In addition, New Age practitioners such as Jean Houston teach that man is still evolving to a new evolutionary level---from *homo sapiens* to *homo noeticus*; and the concept of *homo noeticus*, the god-man, is actively promoted by organizations such as the Institute of Noetic Sciences, led by former NASA astronaut, Ed Mitchell.

Therefore, the Theory of Evolution did not only originate within an occult framework, but is absolutely the key in understanding occult philosophies. For if one fails to realize that occultists believe the universe evolved from a primary energy source which it deems as "god," "the force," or "the mother goddess"---no understanding of occult philosophy will ever be reached. In addition, the occult world holds to the notion that this "energy" or "force" indwells everyone and everything. This all-indwelling force is termed immanence. Immanence is one of the foundational principles of the occult world, and this indwelling force is seen by occultists as the evolutionary impetus that has implemented the cosmic changes that will eventually lead to the emergence of *homo noeticus*—the god-man.

PROMOTION OF EVIL UNDER THE GUISE OF GOOD

There are very few that can imagine a more noble cause than that of serving humanity in order to solve all of the earth's woes. Throughout history, organizations have been formed to promote world peace, feed the hungry, heal the sick, and house the homeless. While many of these organizations and individuals are motivated by honorable motives and many work very hard to achieve their goals; there are many that are not as they appear on the surface—for what better method to camouflage Evil than with good works?

LUCIS TRUST

While many organizations implement this methodology, there exists no better example of this cloaking device than its expert manipulation by the Lucis Trust. Lucis Trust was originally founded in 1922 by theosophists Alice and Foster Bailey as the Lucifer Publishing Company. The name was later changed from Lucifer to Lucis Publishing (for reasons which may occur to you), and was used primarily as the publishing house for Alice Bailey's occult writings. Since that time, Lucis Trust has become a registered NGO of the United Nations with five divisions: The New Group of World Servers, The Arcane School, Lucis Productions, Triangles, and World Goodwill. According to its own promotional literature, the purposes of the Lucis Trust are as follows:

> The world activities of the Lucis Trust are dedicated to the establishment of right human relations. They promote the education of the human mind towards recognition and practice of the spiritual principles and values upon which a stable and interdependent world society may be based.
>
> The Lucis Trust is nonpolitical and nonsectarian. It sponsors no special creed or dogma. The motivating impulse is love of God, expressed through love of humanity and service of the human race. A new and better way of life for all people everywhere in the world can become a reality in our time. Practical techniques in operation today can be learned and applied to the fulfillment of the divine plan for humanity. (8)

Who can argue with the goals of right human relations, a better way of life for all people everywhere, fulfillment of the divine plan for humanity, and with the impulse the love of God? Things look even better if one reads more of the same brochure that describes Word Goodwill and Triangles:

> Triangles was founded in 1937 to stimulate the growth of right human relations by uniting like-minded men and women of goodwill in a spiritual service...World Goodwill was established in 1932. The overall purpose of World Goodwill is the establishment of right human relations through the practical application of the principle of goodwill. (9)

However, a closer inspection of the Lucis Trust literature reveals the deeply occult nature of this organization:

> Lucis Productions produces radio and video programs based on the principles of the Ageless Wisdom. Radio programs include such topics as *meditation, the next world order, spiritual values*, and death and dying...The world has a spiritual destiny. *Behind evolution there is an abiding purpose, we can call the Plan of God.* All who respond to spiritual need can, in their own way and within their own environment, cooperate in fulfilling the divine Plan... (emphasis added) (10)

These quotations taken from the same Lucis Trust brochure begin to reveal the true nature of this organization. The italicized words in the excerpt above are keys to understanding exactly what is intended by the author of this brochure:

- Ageless Wisdom—The Ageless Wisdom referenced here is the equivalent to the "Ancient Mysteries" in the Mystery Religions that began at the Tower of Babel. This "wisdom" or these "mysteries" contain the information communicated to the adepts by a hierarchical group of spiritual beings. It further is communicated by four methods: automatic writing, transcendental meditation, hypnosis, and drugs. These spiritual beings are none other than the fallen angels or demons who inhabit the spiritual realm.
- Alice Bailey--the founder of the Lucis Trust, was the successor to H.P. Blavatsky and Annie Besant. Blavatsky wrote *The Secret Doctrine*, the book that served as Adolf Hitler's "bible" in his attempt to establish a "new world order." *The Secret Doctrine* was written by Blavatsky via "automatic writing" under the direction of a hierarchical master just as Bailey's writings were dictated to her by a "master of wisdom."
- Spiritual Destiny—This is not the destiny of those who are saved as established in the Word of God, but rather an occult interpretation of a coming "spiritual 'Kingdom of God' on earth" that the Bible describes as the kingdom of Antichrist.
- Evolution—as stated previously, the theories of evolution are critical to the occult plan.

- The Plan—"The Plan" is the blueprint for building a new world order is communicated to Blavatsky and Bailey by the demonic Masters of Wisdom.

The revelation of the dark side of the Lucis Trust does not end with this. The initial quotation from the Lucis Trust brochure conveys more than strikes the casual reader when it states, "They promote the education of the human mind towards recognition and practice of the spiritual principles and values upon which a stable and interdependent world society may be based." When these words are read by the discerning individual, the following questions beg to be asked:

- How would this group educate the human mind?
- What are the spiritual principles to be recognized and practiced?
- Whose values should be recognized and practiced?
- What is the definition of an "interdependent world society?"

The answers to these questions are made manifest when one considers the following excerpt from the World Goodwill Newsletter:

> "This is a time of preparation not only for a new civilisation and culture in a new world order, but also for the coming of a new spiritual dispensation. Humanity is not following an uncharted course. There is a divine Plan in the Cosmos of which we are a part. At the end of an age human resources and established institutions seem inadequate to meet world needs and problems. At such a time the advent of a Teacher, a spiritual leader or Avatar, is anticipated and invoked by the masses of humanity in all parts of the world.
>
> Today the reappearance of the World Teacher, the Christ, is expected by millions, not only by those of Christian faith but by those of every faith who expect the Avatar under other names -- the Lord Maitreya, Krishna, Messiah, Imam Mahdi and the Bodhisattva...The coming world Teacher will be mainly concerned, not with the result of past error and inadequacy, but with the

> requirements of a new world order and with the reorganisation of the social structure." (11)

Literature from The New Group of World Servers within World Goodwill provides even more answers:

> "The New Group of World Servers are not however, a band of impractical mystics... They know exactly what they seek to do; they are discovering and bridging together the men and women of goodwill all over the world...'I'hey will conform to and accept the situation in which they find themselves. but will (in that situation and under that government or religious order) work for goodwill, for the breaking down of barriers, and for world peace...they will cultivate the spirit of co-operation, utilizing every opportunity to emphasize the brotherhood of nations, the unity of faith, and economic interdependence.
>
> These are the broad generalities governing the conduct of people of goodwill co-operating in and with the work being done by the New Group of World Servers. They can be regarded as the embodiment of the emerging kingdom of God on earth, but it should be remembered that this kingdom is not a Christian kingdom...or an earthly government. It is a grouping of all those who belonging as they do to every world religion and every nation and race and type of political party are free from the spirit of hatred and separativeness..." (12)

Finally, even if individuals or organizations speak of prayer, the discerning individual must examine exactly what a prayer entails. This is the case with the prayer promoted by Lucis Trust, The Great Invocation:

> "The Great Invocation is a world prayer translated into over fifty languages and dialects, and is used by all triangle members. It expresses certain central truths which all people innately and normally accept; that there exists a basic intelligence to whom we give the name of

> God. That there is a divine Evolutionary Plan in the universe- The motivating power of which is love, that a great individuality called by Christians the Christ-the World Teacher-came to Earth and embodied that love so that we could understand that love and intelligence are effects of the purpose, the will and the Plan of God. Many religions believe in a World Teacher, knowing him under such names as The Lord Maitreya, the Imam Mahdi, and the Messiah, The truth that only through humanity itself can the divine Plan work out." (13)

The quotations listed above are the very essence of the Luciferic plan for whole system transition to a planetary society that Lucis Trust calls a "new world order." This plan is captured in the answers to the questions posed a few paragraphs back:

- How would this group educate the human mind?
  By deception.
- What are the spiritual principles to be recognized and practiced?
  Those on which all of humanity can agree, and around which all can unite.
- Whose values should be recognized and practiced?
  Only those who advocate tolerance and "nonseparativeness."
- What is the definition of an "interdependent world society?"
  A one-world government ruled by "The Christ."

THE ROLE OF THE CHURCH IN ACCOMPLISHING THE GOALS OF THE LUCIS TRUST

The answers to the questions reveal that this so-called "Plan of God" is not consistent with the plan of the true God of the Bible. This "plan," is a strategy to bring peace on the Earth with the revelation of the coming "World Teacher, or the "Christ." One must understand that the term "Christ" is not a reference to one single person, but to the individual who holds the office of the "Christ." Additionally, the occultist believes that many have held the office of the Christ, and Jesus of Nazareth is readily acknowledged by occult sources as one who held this very office. However, by their estimation, he was but one of many so-called "christs" that include the likes of the Lord Maitreya, Krishna, Buddha, Quetzalcoatl, and the Imam Madhi.

In other words, this world teacher heralded by Lucis Trust (as well as other occult religions, individuals, and organizations) is not the returning Jesus Christ who will appear with His saints at the "Second Coming" in fulfillment of God's promises to Israel. Antithetically, a more than cursory reading of the description of the Great Invocation and the information from the New Group of World Servers reveals that this world teacher is none other than Antichrist himself, and that many who mistakenly call themselves "Christian" will embrace the false christ as the true Messiah.

This is the true essence of the Luciferic plan to defeat God, and those "Evangelicals" who are willing to forsake expository doctrinal preaching and the other biblical commands for the structure of the local church as outlined in I Timothy and II Timothy for a new "seeker friendly," purpose-driven, or outcome-based approach to ministry are playing right into the hands of the deceptive plan of the false messiah. As stated by Alice Bailey in her major occultic work, *Externalization of the Hierarchy*:

> "The Christian Church in its many branches can serve as a John the Baptist, as 'a voice crying in the wilderness,' as a nucleus through which world illumination may be accomplished." (14)

How could this be true, and how could those who call themselves "Evangelical" or "Fundamentalist" in reality even accept, much less promote, a Luciferic agenda? There is but one answer to this question: Those who name the Name of Jesus Christ are not immune to deception, and any of this number who do not hold their leaders accountable to the Word of God---or---those who do not know the teachings of the Word of God well enough to hold their leaders accountable—are suspect to the same snare as the childre*n* of Hamlin who blindly followed the seductive melodies of the Pied Piper. For the *Bible* is explicit in its teachings that false teachers will infiltrate the Church and will lead the undiscerning astray. This pattern of apostasy is seen from the Church's earliest days, and the battle to defend the Faith against false teachers is nothing new.

For those older readers of this manuscript who recall the great "Ecumenical Movement" of the 1960s and the mass exodus from mainline Protestant churches, many Bible-believing "Defenders of the Faith" in that period were convinced that the Ecumenical Movement was in fact the "Great End-time Apostasy" described in Scripture. (14) However, when one closely scrutinizes all of the evidence without emotional intervention, the truth of the matter is that the Protestant denominations as a whole were never in complete conformity to the Word of God. Even the most orthodox embraced aspects of Catholicism, and were never pure in their complicity to Scripture.

However, the great warriors of the Faith from the 1930s to the 1970s who defended the Truth and separated from the doctrinal impurity of those who allowed Modernism into their churches, seminaries, and other agencies sought to establish churches of scriptural purity. Tragically, these very churches now face the onslaught of the "Church of the New Paradigm" that threatens to drive the children and grandchildren of formerly stalwart defenders of the Faith to a position of compromise and ultimate apostasy.

This apostasy will not manifest itself by an attack on the great fundamental doctrines of the Faith as did Modernism. As a matter of fact, even the very leaders of the current "church revolution" ostensibly hold to doctrinal positions that even Charles H. Spurgeon would have approved. However, the subtle infusions of "theistic evolution," mysticism, occult terminologies, globalism, behavioral sciences, outcome-based processes, and veiled doctrinal irregularities threaten to destroy the very foundations of the Faith to the point that the "Evangelical" church will implode and collapse upon itself for lack of a solid foundation.

The overwhelming danger of the current assault on Fundamental Christianity is simply the subtlety of the assault. While many may contend this coincidental, a similar plan has manifested itself on the political side of one-world globalism with the goal of establishing another facet of the so-called "new world order." This plan, known as "piecemeal functionalism," was proposed by Richard Gardner in the

April 1973 issue of *Foreign Affairs Magazine,* the publication of the Council on Foreign Relations:

> "In short, the 'house of world order' will have to be built from the bottom up rather than from the top down...an end run around national sovereignty, eroding it piece by piece, will accomplish much more than the old-fashioned frontal assault..." (16)

This same strategy has now been purloined to instigate a "church revolution." That is not to say that the leaders of this revolution are intentionally forsaking conformity to the Word of God, but the facts certainly compel one to seriously question not only their motives, but even their spiritual disposition.

Going back to John MacArthur's assessment of the current situation, the addition of mysticism to doctrinally deprived, seeker sensitive, purpose-driven, outcome-based church growth strategy is the final step toward a major spiritual disaster or broad-based shift. Furthermore, a close scrutiny of the CGM and particularly the "purpose-driven" model reveals an infusion of "creeping occultism" embedded within these programs.

EMBRACING PANTHEISM

Not only did Lucifer lie to Eve when he told her "ye shall not surely die," but he also lied when he said, "ye shall be as gods." The basic premise of pantheism is the godhood of not only man, but everything else as well. The addition of monism rounds out the modern "westernized" version of immanence: God *is everything* and *in everything.* While this concept was foreign to the American mind for almost a century, its arrival in the 1960s initiated changes that would not only permeate, but profoundly influence Western culture. As a matter of fact, the whole of Western culture is relatively new to Eastern religious concepts.

For more than 1200 years, the Roman Catholic Church dominated the culture of Western Europe to the extent that very few individuals possessed any inkling of Eastern Religions. However, when the Church of Rome and Pope Urban II decided to claim the Holy Land for its own property, an unexpected side effect included the introduction of Eastern

Mysticism into the Western psyche. This dubious infusion of occult knowledge was transmitted by knights returning from the Crusades.

The Roman Church reacted to this affront to its dominance by attempting to force the mystics underground or exterminate them entirely. However, in spite of Rome's best efforts, mysticism and occultism triumphed to the degree that launched the occult knowledge manifested in the Renaissance. As a result, along with the Renaissance came the widespread study of Eastern Religions and the occult.

With the Protestant Reformation, an alliance of sorts between the Church of Rome and her wayward protestant offspring confined these studies and philosophies to the intellectual and scientific community or other fringe elements such as "secret societies." The intimate knowledge of the occult would remain, as a general rule, suppressed until the 1960s. In this decade of radical change, the British rock group, *The Beatles*, introduced the "flower generation" to Maharaja Maharish Yogi. This began a new infusion of Eastern mysticism into Western society that mushroomed into the New Age Movement of the late 1970s. As a result, Eastern thought now permeates many facets of western culture, and the principles of pantheism are far and away more prevalent in everyday Western culture than many realize.

While the infusion of monistic pantheism into the broad-based culture is quite disturbing, the introduction of these principles into the Church is far more devastating. In spite of the obvious, Dr. Rick Warren, in his best-selling book, *The Purpose-Driven Life*, makes the statement: "The Bible says, 'He rules everything and is everywhere and is in everything.'" (17) However, does the Bible actually make this statement? As so clearly detailed by Warren Smith in his book, *Deceived on Purpose*, the particular Bible quoted by Dr. Warren does, in fact, make this exact statement. (Dr. Warren seemingly resorts to multiple translations to prove his points.) This particular statement is made based on Ephesians 4:6 in the New Century Version:

> "He rules everything and is everywhere and in everything." (18)

However, a comparison to the King James Version produces quite an anomaly. The KJV renders the same passage:

> "One God and Father of all, who is above all, and through all, and in you all." (19)

The last phrase in this verse is not rendered "in you all" because the Apostle Paul was from southern Tarsus (as those in the southern U.S. would use the phrase "you all"). The text is rendered "in you all" because the Apostle is relating the Biblical principle that the Holy Spirit of God indwells every believer—for the book of Ephesians was written to believers who were members of the Church at Ephesus—not to the world as a whole. Thus, the phrase "in you all" does not state that God is "in everything," but does state the fundamental doctrine of the Scripture that declares that God Himself indwells every believer.

The truth is that God is not "in everything." As the Creator, God is "above all" and therefore possesses power over all of His creation. Mankind is also witness to the power and the might of the Creator by observing the creation. But God does not indwell every atomic fiber of the universe, nor is He some mystical energy force that makes up all of His created works. He is *over the creation,* He *holds His creation together*, but He does not *inhabit the creation*. God only indwells the believer—who as a result, becomes the "temple of the Living God." (20)

Therefore, the principle of the immanence in all creation is not a biblical principle, but rather, a monistic principle. Conclusively, the New Century Version cannot be trusted, and neither can Dr. Warren be trusted. Intentional or unintentional, the concept of immanence is but one aspect by which Dr. Warren is subtly and deceptively injecting pantheistic principles into the Church and accelerating the "creeping occultism" of the New Paradigm Church.

CONCLUSION

The strategy of Lucifer in his war against God is multifaceted. He does indeed use the grotesque and the macabre to influence those whose minds and consciousnesses are seared to the point that they are sold out to an extreme position. He also uses possession, mental oppression, immorality, and criminal activity to initiate the fall of many. In all of these cases, Lucifer successfully presents evil (even extreme evil) as good. Even in the case of "church people," Lucifer appears as the Bible states, "as an angel of light." As so succinctly stated by Warren Smith in his book, *Deceived on Purpose,*

> "The Bible is clear that the truth cannot be mixed with untruth or half-truth when bringing people to the Lord. That's how people end up spiritually deceived." (21)

The primary weapon in Lucifer's arsenal is that of deception, and deception will be the ultimate downfall of those within the New Paradigm Church who attempt fulfill the "Great Commission" by *Rebuilding the Tower of Babel.*

ENDNOTES

(1) Houston, Jean. "*Whole System Transition and the Move to a Planetary Society*", Audio Tape of speech given to The Association of Supervision and Curriculum Development, 1989.
(2) II Thessalonians 2:11
(3) MacArthur, John. *Reckless Faith,* Crossway Books, 1994, pp.154-155.
(4) Warren, Rick. "*The State of the Church,*" DVD, Saddleback Community Church, October 2004.
(5) Taylor, Ian. *In the Minds of Men: Darwin and the New World Order,*TFE Publishing, Minneapolis, MN, 1991, pp.77-79,130-132.
(6) Ibid. p.78.
(7) Ibid.
(8) Lucis Trust promotional brochure. Lucis Publishing, New York, 1996.
(9) Ibid.
(10) Ibid.
(11) World Goodwill Newsletter, "The Purpose of World Goodwill," Lucis Trust, New York, 1998.
(12) The New Group of World Servers. Promotional Brochure, World Goodwill, New York.

(13) Ibid.
(14) Bailey, Alice. *The Externalization of the Hierarchy*, Lucis Trust, New York, 1932, p.510.
(15) II Timothy 3:1-5.
(16) Gardner, Richard. "The Hard Road to World Order", *Foreign Affairs*, April 1974.
(17) Warren, Rick. *The Purpose-Driven Life*, Zondervan Publishing, Grand Rapids, MI, 2002, p.88.
(18) Ephesians 4:6 KJV
(19) Ephesians 4:6 *New Century Version*. Ft. Worth, Texas: Worthy Publishing, 1987.
(20) This principle is discussed at length by Warren Smith in his book, *Deceived on Purpose*.
(21) Smith, Warren. *Deceived on Purpose*, Conscience Press, Ravenna, Ohio, 2004, p.162.

Chapter 2

Witchcraft in the Church?

There are many events in life that appear a complete paradox, but even the slightest whisper of witchcraft imbedded in a "Christian" assembly immediately results in outcries of disbelief, denial, or even abject horror. This is due to the fact that the perceptions of the Church (as well as broad-based concepts of witchcraft across the general population) will not allow any mental accommodation of a logical synthesis of witchcraft and true Christianity. Additionally, the vast majority of Christians would not recognize witchcraft even if it actually did exist within their local assemblies.

However, as stated in Chapter 1, from the early days of the Church, the New Testament reveals that false teachers successfully made clandestine infiltrations of local Christian assemblies; and if the early Church could be deceived by Gnosticism and other forms of occult beliefs-- what makes the modern Church immune from such deception as witchcraft? Taking into consideration the widespread ignorance and general misconceptions regarding witchcraft, a detailed discussion of witchcraft must be addressed as prerequisite to any examination of occult infusions into local assemblies.

ORIGINS OF WITCHCRAFT

The unorganized nature of witchcraft necessitates that the most reliable estimates of the numbers of participating individuals originate from surveys taken by organizations within "the craft." However reliable these statistics may or may not be, there is no doubt of the explosive growth witnessed in the last two decades of the numbers of individuals involved in pagan rituals, occult practices, witchcraft in general, and Wicca in particular. One such poll taken in July of 1999 by Covenant of the Goddess (CoG) reported the number of witches and pagans in the United States as approximately 768,400. This survey also reported 65% of pagan adherents as between the ages of 18 and 39 years and 71% female. (1) In spite of the burgeoning popularity of witchcraft, there is much debate and confusion not only concerning its origins, but also as to the particular belief system of that which denotes a true witch.

The Bible defines a witch as an individual who utilizes sorcery to manipulate events, contact the dead, or fraternize with "familiar spirits." (Familiar spirits are known in New Age circles today as "Spirit Guides.") As the afore-mentioned survey indicated, today's modern witches are a segment of the broader demographic generally classified as "pagan" or "neo-pagan." In the current postmodern society, pagans and neo-pagans are generally viewed as benign, "tree-hugging," hippie-type nature lovers. However, a thorough study of pagan and occult religious practices from the past not only reveals widespread demonic and satanic influence, but also the permeation of satanic "black magick" in ancient witchcraft itself.

Conversely, neo-pagans insist that that the word *pagan* (a term derived from the concept of a country dweller or a back woods "hick") was a derogatory term coined by the medieval Church of Rome to further denigrate not only those who rebelled against its ecclesiastical hierarchy but also as a means of the further suppression of women. While this concept may well be based on a measure of truth, any attempt by the neo-pagan community to appropriate the concepts of Catholicism used by the church to advance its own agenda does not constitute any conclusive proof of an absence of demonic activity within paganism or witchcraft. In essence, any such contention is either a naïve misconception or a thinly veiled untruth.

In conjunction with this line of reasoning, most modern witches consider witchcraft a pantheistic or polytheistic nature religion ostensibly based on older pagan religions. Neo-pagans attempt to retain the basic aspects of ancient paganism while discarding the elements of these religions that they deem as no longer plausible. In other words, most modern witches and other neo-pagans have developed a homogenized, sanitized, politically correct version of the ancient religions that formerly incorporated such practices as animal or human sacrifice, bestiality, ceremonial castration, cannibalism, and sanctified prostitution that were demanded by the Goddess and her consort in years past.

Therefore, the key to understanding modern witchcraft is to grasp the concept of the Mother Goddess. Once this aspect is incorporated in the equation, the modern witch is clearly seen as one who is involved in a fertility nature religion where all of nature is seen as divine, and "Mother Earth" or Gaia is a living, breathing entity who must be worshipped. As revealed by Johanna Michaelson in the book, *Like Lambs to the Slaughter*:

> "Some Witches trace their traditions to the myths of the ancient Greeks and Romans; others, to the Egyptians, Sumerians, the Norse gods of the Vikings, or to the ancient Celts. Still others cheerfully blend any number of traditions and sources together, including bits and pieces from modern science fiction and fantasy (Star Trek and Tolkien's Ring Trilogy are among the most popular), to create their own unique interpretation and set of rituals." (2)

Margot Adler, professed witch and feminist, in her book *Drawing Down the Moon: Witches, Druids, Goddess-Worshippers, and other Pagans in America Today*, quotes Dallas witch, Morgan McFarland:

> "I see myself as monotheistic in believing in the Goddess, Creatrix, the Female Principle, but at the same time acknowledging that other gods and goddesses do exist through her as manifestations of her, facets of the whole." (3)

There are many dangers in the pursuit of this holistic, neo-pagan goddess worship. In the first place, the basic world view of the neo-pagan, as seen in the quotation by Morgan MacFarland, is the type of pantheism termed as *panentheism*—(this aspect will be discussed later in this chapter, but MacFarland incorrectly calls this monotheism.) This world view will not only lead one to a deeper rejection of the Word of God and Jesus Christ as the savior of the world, but also to acceptance of the "doctrines of devils" proclaimed by the spirit guides accessed within goddess worship.

Even more ominous is the attraction of the overtly satanic or "dark side" of these philosophies. While any embracing of pantheism without future repentance will condemn the adherent to an eternity in hell, embracing the "dark side" of occult philosophy will in all probability prove deadly not only to the adherent but also to many with whom these individuals come in contact. Examples of such individuals who sold out to the "dark side" (other than Darth Vader) include rocket scientist Jack Parsons (who claimed to be Antichrist), Aleister Crowley (in his time, known as the most evil man in the world), Albert Pike, Adolf Hitler, and the infamous Charles Manson.

EVOLUTION OF THE MODERN WITCH

The lines of argument are then set. If a neo-pagan in the Wiccan religion claims no relationship to Lucifer, insists there is no real Devil, and believes in the Mother Goddess—is this individual a witch or not? Furthermore, were those who claimed to be witches in the past cast in this same mold, or did they actually profess to worship Lucifer? The truth of the matter is easily discovered. The religion of witchcraft has progressed from its former position of evil spells, attacks utilizing paranormal forces, animal sacrifice, human sacrifice, and even the worship of Lucifer to a kinder, gentler, civilized, politically correct witchcraft—just as mainline, liberal Protestantism has been molded by the modern culture. A study of this evolution of witchcraft is very enlightening.

The modern consensus of a witch was cast in 1484 with the publication of *Hammer of the Witches*, written by two Dominican monks who were members of the Inquisition. According to this publication, witchcraft was a heresy conspiring to overthrow the Church of Rome and establish the kingdom of Satan on Earth. "By their own confessions, they (witches) flew on demonic horses or broom-sticks, they feasted, danced and copulated with each other, with their familiar spirits, and sometimes the devil himself...witches made a formal pact with the devil." (4)

This perception of witchcraft made its way to the New World and was succinctly recorded by eyewitnesses to the Salem Witchcraft Trials in New England in 1692. In a nutshell, the testimonies of these trials reveal several facts:

- Many who were tried, convicted and executed for the crime of witchcraft were innocent victims.
- However, the evidence reveals that all were certainly not innocent, and there is indisputable evidence of crimes to the extent murder committed that involved the manipulation of paranormal forces.
- The confession of William Barker in the Salem trials claimed there were 307 witches scattered throughout New England, and they were involved in a plot to replace Christianity in the New World with Devil Worship. (5)

The witchcraft of Salem and pre-Colonial Europe does not, however, ring true with the modern, sanitized, 21st Century version of witchcraft popularly and publicly displayed as Wicca. Wiccans generally point back to the 1940s and Gerald Gardner for their brand of witchcraft; and they claim this to be the true, ancient witchcraft of all ages. Actually, Gardner began studying and writing on witchcraft rituals of ancient times and pulled bits and pieces of that which he discovered to formulate what many today call Wicca. (6) Most Wiccans, however, are completely unaware of the fact that many of Gardner's rituals were actually written by none other than the notorious "black magick" Satanist, Aleister Crowley after Gardner became an initiate in Crowley's *Ordo Templi Orientis*. (7)

Paradoxically, the great majority of Wiccans will insist that they do not believe in Satan or a Devil as such, but they worship the Mother Goddess as revealed in nature. Most hold to a "Star Wars" style of religion that dictates oneness, interconnection, immanence, and community as the aspects of the goddess (This will be discussed in detail later). (8) Since they (and everything else) are one with and manifestations of the goddess, they attempt to go inside themselves and discover the goddess within-- and thus reach their full human potential.

In somewhat of another contradiction, most will tell you that the consort of the goddess is the mythical god, Pan. (Most pagan and neo-pagan religions worship or acknowledge the existence of many gods as manifestations of the goddess.) Pan is revealed in folk lure as the horned half-man, half goat; or even is portrayed as the satyr—the upper torso of a man with the lower body of a horse. Pan is the god of the underworld or the "god of the hunt." The description of Pan equates to Osiris in the Egyptian Mysteries, Bacchus in the Babylonian Mysteries, Baal of Old Testament fame, and can be traced directly to Nimrod, who the Bible describes as "a mighty hunter against the Lord," (9) and the builder of the Tower of Bàbel. David Livingstone records:

> "In medieval times, the devil was known as the Goat of Mendes...According to (the Egyptian Mysteries and documented by *ed.*) Plutarch, after Set dismembered Osiris' body, his penis was never found, and Isis made a gold replica of it and buried it at Mendes, where there was a temple to the goat god. Plutarch noted that the most beautiful women were selected to lie with the divine Goat of Mendes." (10)

Most interestingly, Mendes is the Egyptian name for both Pan and for a goat. Therefore, when a modern witch admits the recognition of Pan as consort to the Goddess, this is an admission (whether realized or not) of the satanic origins of a religion that paradoxically and emphatically denies the existence of Lucifer.

When taken to its logical conclusions, one must reasonably question the correlation between the Mother Goddess and Lucifer. If the Mother Goddess has Pan as her consort, is Pan not just another manifestation of Lucifer himself? Where then did the worship of the Mother Goddess originate?

The Bible itself records in the Old Testament the worship of Ashteroth, Astarte, Isis, the "Queen of Heaven," and other female variations of goddess worship. *The reality is that modern witchcraft had its origins at the Tower of Babel,* and the infusion of the worship of mother goddess and the "mother and child cults" evidenced throughout world religions for the last 4500 years were conceived in the Babylonian Mysteries that originated with the widow of Nimrod, Semiramis and the "son of the widow," Tammuz.

Variations and cults derived from goddess worship and the Mystery Religions even influenced Judaism. The Jews were heavily influenced by the occult world when they developed an "oral mystical interpretation" of the Old Testament known as the Kabbalah:

> "Although falsely claiming to date from some time prior to the Flood, the system of the Kabbalah represented the appropriation of foreign doctrines into Judaism adopted by the Jews in the great ancient city of Babylon, when they were held there in captivity in the early part of the sixth century, BC." (11)

The Kabbalah is among the direct ancestors of Gnosticism, and with the advances of the Moors into Europe in the Ninth Century, magical and mystical cults fleeing into southern Europe brought with them a Gnostic dualism that directly led to the worship of Lucifer. (12) According to David Livingstone:

> "They worshipped Lucifer, regarding the material world as his work, and holding that by indulging in carnal pleasures they were accommodating their Demon-Creator. It was said that a black cat figured in their ceremonies as an object of worship...at their nocturnal orgies, sacrifices of children were made and their blood used for making the Eucharistic bread of the sect." (13)

WHITE MAGICK VS. BLACK MAGICK

Thus witchcraft, with its origin at the Tower of Babel has evolved from the open worship of Lucifer to the modern sanitized version of the craft—Wicca. However, like a ghoulish, haunting specter, the underlying issue in Wicca and other "white magick" neo-pagan belief systems is the question of the imbedded worship of Lucifer himself lurking under the white-washed façade of the Mother Goddess. The late Anton LaVey, founder and self appointed high priest of the Church of Satan in San Francisco, had a very dogmatic view of this question. In his book, *The Satanic Witch,* he stated:

> "Any girl or woman (LaVey contended that a witch can only be female. –ed.) who claims to practice

only 'Wicca' or 'white magick' is either kidding herself or has much to learn." (14)

In support of this contention, this author received a personal email containing the following statement:

> "Many witches do not even believe in a Satan of any sort. Personally –Satan is my lord and father - I fall into the satanic witch camp!!!! We are for the emancipation of the entire human race from the plunderings of a murdering jewish god---- whom does not exist as such but is merely mass hysteria of the fearful xtians *(sic)* perpetuating their own reality and prophecies on their own humanity and world. It is the actions of teachings of xtianity *(sic)* which hinders the worlds increased development. This will soon end.
>
> All will awaken to the light within soon!!!!" (15)

In the light of history and the above statements, this author must agree (as painful as that may be) with the contention of LaVey. The deceptive nature of Lucifer himself is evidenced in the very fact that those individuals who believe they are seeking the goddess within are outwardly and in reality serving the "god of this world"---Lucifer himself.

THE MOTHER GODDESS AND THE CHURCH

Now that a baseline has been established as to the position of modern witchcraft, the question must be addressed as to its infusion into the Church. As this subject is addressed, several prerequisites and disclaimers must be stated:

- When addressing the Church, this manuscript is speaking only of those who profess salvation by faith in the cleansing blood of Jesus Christ---not those in the Modernist camp who carry only a façade of Christianity.

- All discussions exclude Roman Catholicism, which in and of itself is a bastion of white magick paganism.
- This author is not necessarily accusing any individual or individuals of involvement in practicing witchcraft unless otherwise directly stated.
- The intention of this discussion is to call into question those who either knowingly or unknowingly are interjecting the terminologies and doctrines of devils into the psyche of those who not only profess Christianity but also those who are being evangelized.
- This chapter will specifically discuss aspects of goddess worship infiltrating the Church. Other occult influences such as New Age and Theosophy will be discussed in later chapters.

Now that witchcraft itself has been addressed, the relationship of witchcraft to the Goddess Religion must be closely scrutinized. Again, Margot Adler supplies the basic information necessary to comprehend the relationship of the witch to the Mother Goddess:

> "Witches consider themselves priests and priestesses of an ancient European shamanistic nature religion that worships a goddess who is related to the Mother Goddess in her 3 aspects of maiden, mother, and crone. Many also worship a god related to the ancient horned lord of the animals, the god of the hunt, the god of death, and the lord of the forests." (16)

This description undeniably is a mirror image of modern sanitized witchcraft as has been described in this manuscript— a pantheistic nature religion ostensibly based on older pagan religions. Starhawk the Witch, in her book, *The Spiral Dance,* clearly states the 3 core principles of Goddess Religion:

- Immanence—We are each a manifestation of the living earth.
- Interconnection—We are all linked to the cosmos as part of one living organism.
- Community—The primary focus is not on the individual, but the group. (17)

Immanence and Interconnection will be discussed over the course of the balance of this chapter. However, the entire next chapter will be devoted to a discussion of "Community."

WITCHCRAFT, IMMANENCE, PANTHEISM, & PANENTHEISM

The preceding chapter discussed the infusion of pantheistic philosophies into the Church. The discussion centered on the contention by Dr. Rick Warren in his book, *The Purpose-Driven Life*, where he stated that "God is everywhere and in everything." To reiterate the diagnosis reached in Chapter 1, while Dr. Warren's statement is not conducive to sound biblical doctrine, it does reflect a form of pantheism.

In way of review, pantheistic philosophy teaches that "all is God." This is the doctrine of the strict pantheist. For example, the strict pantheist may state when drinking a glass of milk that "God" is drinking "God" from a glass container that is also "God." For this individual believes that one object is just as much "God" as the other, whether inanimate or living. However, the teaching of witchcraft is not as the strict pantheist, for witchcraft teaches of a transcendent Mother Goddess who exists above all as the guiding energy force of the universe. Furthermore, this teaching contends that all things—whether living or inanimate—are manifestations of the Mother Goddess and are indwelled by the Mother Goddess. Such a belief system is closer to a form of pantheism known as *panentheism.* Laurie Cabot, the ""Official Witch of the State of Massachusetts," confirms this in her book, *Power of the Witch*:

> "... witches believe in their oneness with the source of all life, the Great Mother, and their position as co-creators of the universe." (18)

Panentheism simply states that there exists a transcendent god (or goddess, or energy force) that rules above everything and indwells everything. Panentheism basically exaggerates strict pantheism to the point that there is recognition of a force that transcends above all of creation. In other words, panentheism allows for a deity that is more "god" than is anything else in the universe, though the balance of the universe is a manifestation of and is indwelled by this same "force" known as "god." In addition, most pagan religions teach that individual adepts can ascend to the point to becoming "wholly one" with "the force" or the Mother Goddess.

As a further example, God (the true God) is transcendent and omnipresent, but He is not thoroughly immanent. God is Holy. God transcends above all of His creation. Furthermore, He is omnipresent—He is always present, but in a transcendent fashion. However, He *does not* indwell all of His creation. God is immanent only in the sense that He indwells those and only those who accept by faith the blood sacrifice of His only begotten Son, Jesus Christ. The Bible teaches that all of creation manifests (or reveals) the glory, majesty, and power of the Creator, but the Bible does not teach the panentheistic principle that God is transcendent over *and* indwells all of His creation. Goddess Religion differs from the worship of the true God in that the Mother Goddess, while truly transcendent, also is completely immanent within all of nature.

All of which makes the translation of Ephesians 4:6 in the New Century Version of the New Testament quoted by Dr. Warren more the doctrine of witchcraft than that of the strict pantheist or the Word of God. All that differs from witchcraft and the New Century's rendering of "He rules everything and is everywhere and in everything" is the gender. If the "He" were changed to "She" the result would be a perfect description of the transcendent Mother Goddess.

The current situation in the Purpose-Driven Church Movement is quite a paradox. Would Charles Spurgeon (to choose a name of a famous Baptist preacher completely at random) ever have dreamed that a conservative Baptist preacher would list *Immanence* as God's presence "in everything?" Would Starhawk the Witch, who believes that all individuals are manifestations of the Mother Goddess, ever have imagined that a conservative Southern Baptist preacher would imply the same of the God of the Bible? (For if God is "in" everything as the New Century Version and Dr. Warren state, is not all of mankind inclusive in "everything?") Could anyone have foreseen this scenario? For most biblically grounded, true Christians--- not in their most vivid nightmares would they have imagined such a departure from the Word of God that would open the door to the teachings of witchcraft in the Church.

INTERCONNECTION

Whether an individual involved in "the occult" or witchcraft is a strict pantheist or a panentheist, there are many common denominators in these belief systems. One such major component is the belief in *interconnection.* Starhawk defined the witches view of interconnection with the statement, "We are all linked to the cosmos as part of one living organism." (19) As stated earlier, the individual involved in witchcraft will state that all things animate and inanimate, are manifestations of the Mother Goddess, the life-force of the universe. As a panentheist, the witch believes that all is controlled and directed by the goddess, rather than left to chance. That fact, however, does not preclude those involved in witchcraft from evolutionary theories. Simply stated, their view of evolution is a variation of *theistic evolution,* as they believe the Mother Goddess, though in and of herself a product of evolution, controls the direction of the perceived evolutionary impetus.

As a matter of fact, the entire basis of the occult view of interconnection is based in the misplaced concept of a primordial "Big Bang." Once one considers the logical course of the Big Bang, however illogical the entire theory may be, the concept of interconnection is a reasonable conclusion. The process in this line of thinking would proceed from the idea that according to the Big Bang, the entire universe was formed from one very small, very dense mass of matter. Now if everything, and theoretically everyone, were ancestrally united and contained in this very small mass (most contend it was about the size of a period on this page), then all of mankind and everything else in the universe originated from this common, if not extremely ancient ancestor. If this indeed were the case, every individual would have a physiological and even a psychological interconnection to everyone and everything else.

Taking this concept to the next level, such a belief system logically concludes that all the knowledge of the universe lies dormant within each individual, and the only issue that remains for mankind is to access that knowledge. The belief in the Mother Goddess simply takes the theory of the Big Bang and states that the goddess is the very life-force that evolved from the Big Bang and controls all of nature by manifesting herself in all of nature. As a result, all is one, all is interconnected, all is a manifestation of the Mother Goddess, all is worthy of worship, and by the way—all is still evolving.

The strict pantheist will have basically the same concept of the evolution of man as does the panentheist, but the strict pantheistic view does not allow for a transcendent figure such as the Mother Goddess. The strict pantheist will simply take the view that "if all the knowledge of the universe is contained within me, then I am God. However, I alone am not God, but everything else in the universe is also God, and the impersonal evolutionary impetus will eventually bring all mankind to the next level of evolution, *homo noeticus*. At this, the final stage of evolution for humankind, all mankind will not only realize they are God but will also possess 'God-like' powers."

INTERCONNECTION & GLOBALISM

Based on this discussion, there is absolutely no surprise that many of the leaders of the movements in the Twentieth Century that promoted (or still promote) the mythical and sometimes ostracized New World Order were well-known occultists. A complete list would be impossible to compile, but some of the more recognizable names include:

- Aleister Crowley, organizer of the OTO and known in his time as the most evil man on Earth
- H.G. Wells, author of *The Time Machine* and *War of the Worlds*
- Aldous Huxley, author of *Brave New World*
- Alice Bailey, leader of the Theosophical Society and founder of the Lucis Trust
- Adolf Hitler, attempted to implement an occult New World Order the hard way
- L. Ron Hubbard, author of *Dianetics* and founder of Scientology
- Marilyn Ferguson, author of *The Aquarian Conspiracy*
- Willis Harman, author of *Global Mind Change* and *Insight to the New Age*
- Ervin Lazlo, author of *The Systems View of the World: A Holistic Vision for Our Time*
- Maurice Strong, Former Senior UN Advisor and organizer of the 1992 Earth Summit

- Jean Houston, Expert in Human Potential and Hillary Clinton's personal medium

All of the individuals in this list made great contributions toward a whole system transition to a planetary society. Such a society would replace Judeo-Christian values with pre-Christian pagan values, establish a world government, establish a one-world religion, and install a world ruler. So what's wrong with such a world system?

Once again retracing the steps of mankind to the Tower of Babel, God Himself separated men by changing their languages and thus instituting the nation state. The efforts of men over the course of history to build a world empire have always been accompanied with a false religion and rebellion against God. Perfect examples of these world empires include the Babylonian Empire, the Medo-Persian Empire, the Greek Empire, and the Roman Empire. With each of these empires came a false religious system that incorporated the occult principles still evidenced in the world today. Furthermore, the Bible very clearly teaches that one more world empire is in the future of humanity. This final world empire will mark the end of this very age, and will be ruled by none other than Antichrist himself--- the man whose kingdom will suffer its ultimate defeat at the hands of Jesus Himself at His Second Coming. In addition, Antichrist will become a priest-king, presiding not only over a global kingdom but also an occult one world religion.

The key to the establishment of this New World Order is *interconnection.* As so succinctly stated by occultist, Dr. Jean Houston:

> "Making a difference has never been more critical in a world in which so much can go right or go disastrously wrong. We are the ones who have the most profound task in human history--the task of deciding whether we grow or die. We have an opportunity to play a role in the greatest transition drama the world has seen. In order to do this we must become able to access depths of body, of mind and spirit that we may have forgotten we had.... *The present emerging ecology of minds and psyches, our availability to each other, our ability to dream each other's dreams and experience each other's*

> *biographies is part of the interpenetrating wave of the current time, psyche, and memory. We are being rescaled to planetary proportions, as we become resonant and intimate with our own depths.* (emphasis added –ed.)
>
> We glimpse in this new century *the coming of a planetary society which heralds the end of ancient enmities and the birth of new ways of using our common humanity and its various cultures*. In fact, we will need a gathering of the potentials of the whole human race and the particular genius of every culture if we are going to survive our time." (20)

In other words, if the human race is to survive and continue to evolve to the next level of evolution, it must access the goddess within each individual and interconnect through each other's dreams, psyches, and memories in order to solidify the reality of a new global society.

Thus interconnection is the very essence of globalism---a planetary society based on occult principles and ultimately the worship of Lucifer. The Bible expressly states, "...and they worshipped the Dragon who gave power to the Beast." (21) The "Beast" is Lucifer's servant, Antichrist (who will be possessed by Lucifer himself), and who will lead the consummate act of rebellion toward Almighty God.

Therefore, any reference to the New World Order is intrinsically if not overtly linked to modern witchcraft and the worship of the Mother Goddess. Just as Starhawk stated that the principle of interconnection signifies the connection of the entire human race to one another as well as to the cosmos as a major tenant of goddess worship, it is also the underlying impetus toward a New World Order and the ultimate reign of Antichrist.

RICK WARREN'S WORLD CLASS CHRISTIAN

Chapter 38 of Dr. Rick Warren's book, *The Purpose-Driven Life,* is titled "How to Become a World Class Christian." The chapter is based on fulfilling the "Great Commission"—Christ's directive to go into all the world and preach the Gospel. The author of this manuscript is in full agreement with this premise, and furthermore, agrees with Dr. Warren that the Church has failed miserably in following this commandment. Every Christian should not only have a burden for lost individuals world-wide, but each individual believer should be fulfilling this commission in whatever manner the Lord has given the capacity to perform its fulfillment.

However, there are some very disturbing aspects of Dr. Warren's appeal to "go into all the world." These concerns are outlined as follows:

- As a prerequisite, in Chapter 36 of *The Purpose-Driven Life*, Dr. Warren relayed to his readers and those using the book as a devotional study guide that Jesus told His disciples not to worry about His return to the earth, but to concentrate on their mission (i.e. The Great Commission). He further discouraged the study of Bible Prophecy by taking the words of Jesus out of context when Dr. Warren stated, "If you want Jesus to come back sooner, focus on fulfilling your commission, not figuring out Bible prophecy." (22)

In light of the discussions here, there are several issues with Dr. Warren's statements that must be addressed as prerequisites to the overall conclusion:

- A full one third of the Bible is prophetic Scripture. Are Christians to tear these pages out of the Bible? This author's Bible states, "*All* Scripture is given by the inspiration of God, and is profitable for doctrine, correction, reproof, and instruction in righteousness. That the man of God may be perfect, thoroughly furnished to all good works." (23) In Dr. Warren's view should the phrase "except those that pertain to Bible prophecy" be added to this verse?
- The Bible is the only holy book of the world's major religions that dares to predict the future. Furthermore, not only does it dare to predict---it does so with 100% accuracy. By this fact alone, the study of Bible prophecy proves to the student of the Word of God that God is indeed the one true God. To discount

Bible prophecy is to discount both the omniscience and omnipotence of God.

- Most significantly in reference to this particular study, an ignorance of Bible prophecy results in an ignorance of the dangers of globalism, the so-called New World Order, and the overt moves toward a One-World Religion.

The bottom line is that an individual cannot recognize error if that same individual is ignorant of the truth. Concerns over terminologies and marketing tactics that are consistent with the terminologies and teachings of witchcraft or goddess worship will go unnoticed when one has no firm grasp of the truth of the "whole counsel of God." This exact scenario would clearly be the case as one considers other aspects of *The Purpose-Driven Life:*

- The second subheading used in Chapter 38, "How to Become a World Class Christian" is *Shift from local thinking to global thinking.* This cute little catch phrase is very much akin to the popular slogan of the radical environmentalists, "Act Locally, Think Globally" and tends to frame the thought process of Dr. Warren's "World Class Christian" along these same lines.
- The next sentence states, "God is a global God." God is far more than just a "global God." God is an infinite, omnipresent, omnipotent God. However, without proper instruction in Bible prophecy and recognition of the dangers of globalistic programs, individuals, and organizations; this statement has the potential of leading the novice to support programs such as the Earth Summit, The Earth Charter, Man and the Biosphere, The Baca Ranch, etc.----just because "God is a Global God."
- Dr. Warren then states that "much of the world already thinks globally." Yes, especially those are working for a one world government, a one world religion, and those who ascribe to a neo-pagan pantheistic world view. Are Christians to join with these groups?

As dangerous as these statements are, a few sentences later Dr. Warren boasts, *"We are more connected than we realize."* (23) Now it is absolutely true that genuine Christians are interconnected to one another as members of the "Body of Christ" through the bond of the

Holy Spirit of God. However, it was not in this context that Dr. Warren made this statement. He stated this after speaking of world trade and the number of countries in which your clothes were manufactured. Occultist Jean Houston, in her 1989 speech, *Whole System Transition: The Move to a Planetary Society*, made exactly the same analogy when explaining that all individuals are interconnected "world beings."

Dr. Jean Houston worships the Mother Goddess. Dr. Jean Houston ascribes to the aspects of the goddess outlined by Starhawk the Witch: Immanence, Interconnection, and Community. This manuscript has detailed that modern witchcraft perceives itself as the religion of the Mother Goddess. Dr. Houston would have no issues identifying with modern witchcraft or Wicca, but what about a "conservative" Baptist preacher? What would be the motive of a preacher who even through ignorance introduces the principles of witchcraft into the Church? Would such an individual have issues identifying with witchcraft? One would certainly hope such an individual would have many issues with such identification; but yet this manuscript has previously exhibited that Dr. Warren's book has promoted an occult form of immanence, and now he touts interconnection. Surely, this must be completely coincidental—or is it?

Lest any misunderstand, this author is not accusing Dr. Warren of practicing or *knowingly* promoting witchcraft in the church. However, as coincidences (if they are in fact coincidences) continue to pile up, one must certainly *question* the true direction (as well as the source) of the methods and teachings of Dr. Warren and the thousands of other pastors pursuing the growth and success of the "Purpose-Driven Church." While a final assessment cannot be made at this juncture, one must conclude that serious problems exist in a religious movement that overtly claims to be fulfilling the Great Commission while in reality is *Rebuilding the Tower of Babel.*

ENDNOTES

(1) www.cog.org/cogpollfinal.html
(2) Michaelson, Johanna. *Like Lambs to the Slaughter*, Harvest

(3) House, Eugene, OR, 1989, Appendix: "The Beliefs of Witches."
(4) Adler, Margot. *Drawing Down the Moon: Witches, Druids, Goddess-Worshippers, and other Pagans in America Today*, rev. ed., Boston, Beacon Press, 1986, p.viii.
(5) Livingstone. *The Dying God*, Writer's Club Press, New York, 2002, p.289.
(6) Lavenda, Peter. *Sinister Forces*, TrineDay, Walterville, OR, 2005, p.29.
(7) Skarrit, Kelly. "Wicca: Modern Day Witchcraft," Community Voice, 5.19.05, p.10.
(8) Lavenda. p.305.
(9) Starhawk. *The Spiral Dance: A Rebirth of the Ancient Religion of the Great Goddess*, (2nd Edition), Harper and Row, San Francisco, 1989, pgs.10-11.
(10) Genesis 10:8-9.
(11) Livingstone. p.291.
(12) Ibid. p.3.
(13) Ibid. p.287.
(14) Ibid.
(15) LaVey, Anton. *The Satanic Witch*, Feral House, Los Angeles, CA, 1970, p.8.
(16) Personal Email. Received Monday, May 01, 2000 7:28 PM.
(17) Adler. pgs.10-11.
(18) Starhawk.
(19) Cabot, Laurie & Cowan, Tom. *Power of the Witch*, Delta, New York, 1989, pgs.10,11, 20.
(20) Houston, Jean. Jean Houston Website, "I invite you to attend a Special Preview of the 2006 Mystery School: The Mystery of Making a Difference," www.jeanhouston.org.
(21) Revelation 13:4.
(22) Warren, Rick. *The Purpose-Driven Life*, Zondervan, Grand Rapids, MI, 2002, p.286.
(23) II Timothy 3:16.
(24) Warren. p.300.

Chapter 3

The Religious Essence of Community

Dr. Rick Warren's assessment of those who attempted to construct the Tower of Babel (see *Introduction)* was absolutely correct. Those individuals were highly motivated to accomplish an impossible task that could only be achieved if they transformed their individual energies into a cohesive unit whereby individuals functioned in complete concert. However, Dr. Warren failed to note the fact that the circumstances described in Genesis 11 indicate that this cohesive unit was empowered by a supernatural force that was in direct opposition to God's desired direction for mankind. Additionally, the building of the Tower of Babel became the basis of what was to become the Babylonian Empire---a world kingdom---the exact opposite of the political direction ordained by God.

These are absolute indicators that the power source behind this construction project was none other than Lucifer himself, and this or any subsequent attempt for the formation of a world government or a world religion is also in direct defiance of God. This defiance was illustrated by the world kingdoms explicitly portrayed in the book of Daniel, and this and other Bible prophecies are very clear that the next world government and world religion will be under the jurisdiction of Antichrist himself. Thus, any support of globalist philosophies or programs (political or religious) must be perceived as the promotion and endorsement of the cause of Lucifer.

In spite of all of this, Dr. Warren used this event as an illustration in his series, *40 Days of Community* as what can be accomplished when men and women work together "in community." Furthermore, Dr. Warren uses this same "community concept" to make the point that Christians must work together as a group to fulfill God's purposes for their lives. He has gone so far as to state, *"You cannot fulfill God's purposes for your life by yourself...you need a group."* (1) However, such tampering with the context of the Word of God in an attempt to make a point also opens the door to intrusions by deceptive Luciferic philosophies upon philosophies upon the sacred text of Scripture. As was revealed in the previous chapter, witchcraft is one such philosophy.

The three cornerstones of the pyramidal foundation of witchcraft and the worship of the Mother Goddess were outlined in the previous chapter. As detailed in Chapter 2, Starhawk (a professing witch), in her book, *The Spiral Dance,* clearly states the 3 core principles of Goddess Religion:

- Immanence—All human beings are each a manifestation of the living earth.
- Interconnection—All are linked to the cosmos as part of one living organism.
- Community—The primary focus is not on the individual, but the group. (2)

Two of those three cornerstones, *Interconnection* and *Immanence*, were not only discussed at length, but the correlation to the teachings in 40 day programs and the book, *The Purpose-Driven Life* was also explicitly detailed. The final cornerstone of Goddess worship is that of *Community.* This entire chapter has been designated to discuss the religious aspects of this principle found extensively in pagan religions because its insidious roots have spread far beyond the realm of the Mother Goddess and witchcraft into other occult philosophies such as Theosophy and broad-based "New Age" teachings. Now, with the efforts of Dr. Warren and his mentor, Peter Drucker (Dr. Drucker's contribution will be discussed in Chapter 4), this same concept of *community* will permeate the "pop culture" of the "churched" evangelical population.

Therefore, what is the essence of the concept of "community?" Do the principles of "community" parallel the teachings of the Word of God, or do these principles correlate more with occult philosophies of paganism? Is the concept of "community" as taught by Starhawk also a biblical concept? Is the concept of "community" equivalent to Christian fellowship? How is this related to the infusion of occult "groupthink" philosophies on modern western society? Basically, what is the truth?

In order to ascertain the truth, one must resort to the source of all truth---the inspired and inerrant Word of God. The foundation of Christian fellowship and unity is found in the book of Ephesians. Ephesians outlines the concept of the "Church Universal," and the truth concerning the "Body of Christ." This book reveals the "mystery of the Church," relating that Gentiles have been granted access to God through the blood of Jesus Christ, and such access was previously reserved exclusively for Israel. Ephesians then builds the analogy of the church as both the "Body of Christ" and as a vital component in the "Temple of the Living God." These principles are summarized in Ephesians 1:22-23 and Ephesians 2:19-22:

> "... and hath put all things under His feet, and gave unto Him to be the head over all things to the church, which is His body, the fullness of Him that filleth all in all." (3)

> "...Now therefore ye are no more strangers and foreigners, but fellow citizens with the saints, and of the household of God; and are built upon the foundation of the apostles and the prophets, Jesus Christ Himself being the chief corner stone; in whom all the building fitly framed together grow unto a holy temple in the Lord: In whom ye also are builded together for an habitation of God through the Spirit." (4)

These passages complete the analogy of both a "living body" and a perfectly constructed "building." The "living body" is made up the whole of true Christianity that includes every true blood-washed child of God—Jew and Gentile-- who has been born again into the "family of God." The perfectly constructed building described in the book of Ephesians includes not only the "New Testament Saints" who are members of the afore-mentioned "living body," but also those Old Testament saints who looked forward to the perfect sacrifice that would cleanse them *post mortem* from all the sin that the sacrificial blood of bulls and goats merely covered from the eyes of a Holy God. Thus it is this "body" and "building" that make as one those who were before Christ separated as Jew and Gentile; but through the shedding of His blood and the power of His resurrection are, and will be, united as one into the household of God. Additionally, those individual members of the body also are, in and of themselves, a "Temple of the Living God" by the presence of the indwelling Holy Spirit.

COMMUNITY CONCEPTS: BIBLICAL-- OR SOMETHING ELSE?

Thus there is indeed a deep spiritual bond that unites those of like faith into fellowship with the Father and each other via the death and resurrection of the Son and the witness of the indwelling Holy Spirit. However, does this correlate to the concept of "community" as presented by the *40 Days of Community* and *The Purpose-Driven Life*? In order to answer this question, one must closely examine exactly that which the book of Ephesians is teaching.

Is Ephesians teaching that Christians are to foster relationships with other Christians for empowerment or protection? Is the Scripture teaching that since all Christians are integral units in the structure of the Temple of God and the components of the Body of Christ, do they individually lack some secret ingredient for spiritual growth unless they work as a group? Is this Scripture teaching that Christians are to build relationships to bind themselves together to conquer fear, gain strength for daily tasks, face life's trials and issues, and fulfill God's purposes for their lives? Would such an emphasis on relationships, bonding, and interdependence be equated more with the doctrines taught in the book of Ephesians or the concepts of group therapy? Yet, Dr. Warren, in his "40 Days of Community" states the following:

> "You cannot be what God wants you to be by yourself...You cannot fulfill God's purposes by yourself...God's answer to fear is 'community'... *40 Days of Community* is all about building relationships." (5)

Granted, there are biblical principles that teach Christians to "bear one another's burdens," uphold each other in prayer, confess our faults one to another, and other interactions between individuals that will aid them to persevere in their Christian walk. One must also not forget that the child of God is commanded to assemble together with other believers as a member of a local church. However, to state that one cannot be what God wants by himself or herself is not only ludicrous, but blatantly unscriptural. This extra-biblical path continued in the "40 Days of Community" when Dr. Warren stated,

> *"We do not grow* (spiritually) *by just sitting and listening to the Bible, but by doing, sharing, ministry, fellowship...* " (6)

With this statement, Dr. Warren minimizes the importance of the preaching and teaching of the Word of God by subordinating it to interpersonal relationships. This tactic is diametrically opposed to the Word of God that proclaims:

> "For the preaching of the cross is to them that perish foolishness; but unto us which are saved *it is the power of God.*" (7)

Based on just this one text, how can any "man of God" that claims the proclamation of "God's message" subordinate the "power of God" to interpersonal relationships—even if these relationships are based upon fellowship among Christians?

If any doubt remained as to the absence of a biblical foundation in the *40 Days of Community*, the afore-mentioned statement alone should assuage the doubts of even the most accommodating soul. One also must bear in mind that the context in which this statement was made was not in reference to membership in a local church, or even regular attendance in the services of a local assembly. Rather, Dr Warren made this statement in reference to participation in a "small group" –the basic building block of the "meta-church" and the very core philosophy of the Church Growth Movement.

Dear friends, in spite of Dr. Warren's contentions, the moving of the Holy Spirit on hearts through the study of the Word of God is the *primary* method God implements for spiritual growth. If the Church were to adopt Dr. Warren's methodology as the governing foundational principles, the members of the Body of Christ would be ruled by human volition and counsel rather than the direction of the Holy Spirit. Yes, Christian relationships, small groups of friends, and family members can assist to validate, reinforce, and even expound the Word of God---but the Holy Spirit works in the heart through His *living Word* effecting the change of a life. As the author of Hebrews penned under the inspiration of the Holy Spirit:

> "For the Word of God is quick, and powerful, and sharper than any two-edged sword, piercing even to the dividing asunder of soul and spirit, and of the joints and marrow, and is a discerner of the thoughts and intents of the heart."(8)

Therefore, any learned individual regurgitating these same community concepts must be questioned as to the source of such a philosophy. For the philosophy behind such concepts stem from sources other than the Word of God. The sixty million dollar questions then are as follows: What philosophy forms the basis of these and similar statements? Where did the idea of building community originate? What is the true basis and rationale for a *40 Days of Community* program? As will be hereafter illustrated, the possibilities are frightening.

COMMUNITY—FINAL CORNERSTONE IN THE FOUNDATION OF GODDESS WORSHIP

As previously stated, the three core principles of the Mother Goddess and modern witchcraft are Immanence, Interconnection, and Community. (9) All three of these principles go hand–in–hand and fully correlate to each other. For if the Mother Goddess is immanent, then everything and everyone is interconnected through her, and all of life makes up a holistic, interdependent community. If this were truly the case, any sexual, ethical, racial, philosophical, or religious divisions of any genre violate the laws of nature and displease the Mother Goddess.

The philosophy then of witchcraft and the worship of the Goddess clearly promotes an interdependent community of all humanity:

> "Guided by ancient wisdom and present inspiration, we will come together and experience *conscious community* and the healing of our relations with each other and the world... Experience our connections...to the Earth and all Creation." (10)

Since the time of the Tower of Babel, fallen man has exercised his desire to access this ancient wisdom by coming together as a human community. This foundational philosophy of Goddess Worship then manifested itself in the Mystery Religions of Babylon and progressed into the teachings of Kabbalism and Gnosticism. This is illustrated in the statement by Tim Wallace-Murphy in his book, *Cracking the Symbol Code* when he stated,

> "The Templars (the Knights Templar of *National Treasure* fame –ed.), being Gnostic initiates, did not concern themselves with the salvation of individual souls, but were mainly concerned with the spiritual and material transformation of entire communities and nations." (11)

Those readers who are familiar with this author's first book, *Outcome-Based Religion: Purpose, Apostasy, and the New Paradigm Church,* may well understand the gravity of this statement. For the "Father of the Church Growth Movement," Donald McGavaran—professor at Dr. Rick Warren's alma mater, Fuller Theological Seminary, and praised by Dr. Warren-- developed what he called the Homogenous Unit Principle (HUP). The HUP de-emphasized individual salvation and emphasized the simultaneous Christian conversion of entire communities. Thus, based on the information conveyed by Mr. Wallace-Murphy, the Father of the Church Growth Movement aligned his views of conversion more with the Gnosticism of the Knights Templar than the teachings of the New Testament.

Dr. McGavaran took his philosophies of church growth to Fuller, and there instilled his group-think philosophies that would lay the foundation for the principles of Goddess Worship and Gnosticism to gain a subliminal foothold within "Evangelical Christianity." These philosophies are now mass-marketed by Dr. Warren and the other Fuller graduates within the CGM who base their methodologies on these principles.

As in the theory behind Dr. McGavaran's Homogenous Unit Principle, the primary *emphasis* of "community" in the religion of the Mother Goddess involves the *de-emphasis* of the individual and the elevation and *exultation of the group*. This group-think concept is also the basis of all evolutionary thought and radical environmentalism—*species survival supersedes individual rights.*

This concept is blatantly illustrated with the *"Declaration of Interdependence"* presented at the 1992 Earth Summit at Rio de Janeiro:

> "This we resolve... At this turning point in our relationship with Earth, we work for an evolution: from dominance to partnership; from fragmentation to connection; from insecurity, to interdependence." (12)

To make matters worse, The Declaration of Interdependence in 1992 was actually the *second* such document by the same title. The first *Declaration of Interdependence* appeared in 1975 when Henry Steele Commager authored a U.N. declaration by that title. It was signed on July 4th, 1976 in Philadelphia and was funded by the Ford Foundation. Over 160 members of Congress signed this declaration. The wording of this *Declaration of Interdependence* was very interesting:

> "...We must join with others to bring forth a *new world order*.... Narrow notions of national sovereignty must not be permitted to curtail that obligation....To establish a *new world order* of compassion, peace, justice and security, it is essential that mankind free itself from the limitations of national prejudice, and acknowledge that the forces that unite it are incomparably deeper than those that divide it, that all people are part of *one global community*, dependent on one body of resources, bound together by the ties of a common

> humanity and associated in a common adventure on the planet Earth." (13)

Congresswoman Marjorie Holt of Maryland refused to sign the Declaration, saying:

> "It calls for the surrender of our national sovereignty to international organizations. It declares that our economy should be regulated by international authorities. It proposes that we enter a *'new world order'* that would redistribute the wealth created by the American people." (14)

Though Congresswoman Holt was absolutely correct in her assessment of the *Declaration of Interdependence* from a political perspective, the two overwhelming dangers behind this document are exactly those of the second *Declaration of Interdependence:*

- These documents promote the pantheistic or panentheistic world view of the Goddess religion creeping into the traditional Judeo-Christian values system of western society. This revived values system not only has resulted in a profound influence on secular society; but thanks to Dr. McGavaran and his followers—the influence of pagan values on the pop culture of "churched" Evangelicals has been overwhelming.
- This group-think model of "community" is laying the foundation for the ultimate global rebellion against God--a "new world order" and the rise of Antichrist himself.

Coincidentally, Rick Warren, in his *40 Days of Community* presentation declared:

> "This is our *Declaration of Interdependence*—I need a group!" (15)

Now why would a conservative Southern Baptist preacher use the same terminology as those who are engaged in Goddess worship or political globalism? At the very least, one must question Dr. Warren's wisdom in opening yet another door for criticism---On the other hand, it almost seems as if Dr. Warren is sending a message to those who understand exactly what the true *Declaration of Interdependence* documents signified when assigning this terminology to an intra-church campaign. If this is the case, Dr. Warren would be sending a signal of ulterior motives and workings behind a façade of conservative Christianity.

COMMUNITY & THE NEW AGE MOVEMENT

The New Age Movement grew out of the drug culture of "flower children" in the 1960s. This anti-establishment generation rebelled against many aspects of western society, and their search for an anti-establishment religion was rewarded when *The Beatles* introduced eastern religion into western thought. Additionally, through the use of mind-expanding drugs, a greater reality (or rather, a greater fantasy) was screaming the siren call for explanations other than that which traditional religion could give; and traditional western concepts of God and love were superseded with the messages transmitted by spiritual forces accessed on drug "trips." As a result, Transcendental Meditation, self-realization, and yoga began to become established on a broad base, and the New Age Movement was born.

In 1980, the New Age Movement received its own "Bible," *The Aquarian Conspiracy*, authored by Marilyn Ferguson. It was in this major New Age treatise that Ms. Ferguson established the concept of "community" as a New Age philosophy. She actually defined the modern concept of community when she stated:

> "The discovery of our connection to all other men, women, and children joins us to another family. Indeed, seeing ourselves as a planetary family struggling to solve its problems, rather than as assorted people and nations assessing blame or exporting solutions could be the ultimate shift in perspective...We think of ourselves separate rather than part of the whole. This imprisons our affection to those few nearest us. Our task must be to free ourselves from this prison by widening our circle to embrace all living creatures... " (16)

With this virtual definition of "community," Ms. Ferguson incorporated the principle of *interconnection* as a vital component in the community-building process. It is this holistic world view that embraces pagan concepts thousands of years old and inserts them into the modern psyche. She then successfully integrated the life-blood of the sexual revolution and the sacred sex of Goddess worship with the concept of interconnection to produce the final formula for "community:"

> "The worldwide quest for community typified by the networks of the Aquarian Conspiracy is an attempt to boost that attenuated power (the power of love and fraternity). To cohere. To kindle wider consciousness. When man reclaims this energy source, the sublimation of spiritual-sensual love...he will have once again discovered fire." (17)

Additionally, Ms. Ferguson ushered the pagan philosophies into the modern religious arena by appealing to the world's religious leaders:

> "The crises of our time are challenging the world religions to release a new spiritual force transcending religious, cultural, and national boundaries into a new consciousness of the human community." (18)

This statement brings the darkest secret for the "evangelical" quest for community into the bright light of day. The call for community internally will naturally evolve to a quest for community externally—"Today we promote a spirit of community in our own church, tomorrow we promote a spirit of community with all of mankind." As a matter of fact, with Dr. Warren's P.E.A.C.E. Plan, one can almost see this very concept on the horizon. In promoting the P.E.A.C.E. Plan, Dr. Warren speaks of "waging peace." Once again, the words of Marilyn Ferguson from *The Aquarian Conspiracy* echo with the very purpose-driven terminology behind Dr.Warren's sales pitch:

> "If we reframe the problem—if we think of *fostering community,* health, innovation, *purpose*– we are already *waging peace*." (19)

Before the reader begins to speculate that this may indeed be a great plan for humanity, the principles of the Word of God must be closely examined:

- The Bible teaches that there is no such thing as a "human community." The Bible is very clear that two distinct groups of individuals reside on the planet: The *saved* and the *lost.*
- Moreover, these two groups are not bound together by a common humanity. The Bible succinctly teaches that the *saved* are the "children of God," (Romans 8:14-17) and the *lost* are "of your father, the Devil." (John 8:44)
- Any effort to establish community among these two groups in any religious cause is contrary to the teachings of the Word of God.

In *The Aquarian Conspiracy,* Ms. Ferguson is promoting this human community via a one world religion under the Mother Goddess, but this author is in no fashion suggesting that *40 Days of Community* or Rick Warren's P.E.A.C.E. Plan insinuates that Christians join in such an occult effort. However, the implementation of the New Age principles and terminology of *the Aquarian Conspiracy* in devotional books and intra-church campaigns is, at a minimum, subliminally preparing those in evangelical churches to embrace the methodology that will be used in building the one world religion and the one world government of Antichrist.

The tragedy of the similarities of the Church Growth Movement and the New Age Movement are staggering. When one reads *The Aquarian Conspiracy* and then reads *The Purpose-Driven Life* by Dr. Rick Warren, it almost seems that *The Purpose-Driven Life* is nothing more than a "Christianized" version of *The Aquarian Conspiracy.* The concepts are similar or identical, the terminology is identical, the individuals quoted by Dr. Warren often held to the same or similar philosophies as those quoted by Marilyn Ferguson (both books positively quote occultist Aldous Huxley), and the three foundational principles of the Mother Goddess and modern witchcraft---*Immanence, Interconnectedness, and Community*--- are prominently evident in both works. To that end, in the fifth installment of *40 Days of Community*, Dr. Warren declared that as was the case with the construction crew at the Tower of Babel, *"... together can do anything.*" Once again, this statement was just as scripted by Marilyn Ferguson when she wrote:

> "As rich as we are—*together we can do anything* to heal our homeland, the Whole Earth." (20)

COMMUNITY AND THE OCCULT WORLD

With the insertion in Ms. Ferguson's quotation regarding the "Whole Earth," the door is opened to the occult aspects of group-think philosophies. As was discussed in Chapter 1, the idea of the preservation of the "group" over individual rights is based in occult thought and manifested in evolutionary theories. When Darwinism was thrust upon the public psyche in the 1920s via the Scopes Trial, the group-think philosophy spread its tentacles into the world view of public perception. Over the last eighty years, the idea of "species survival" suddenly overshadowed concepts of the nation state, individual rights, and even individual salvation.

This same philosophy has now infiltrated evangelicalism and fundamentalism with the rise of the "meta-church." The meta-church concept was presented by another product of Fuller Theological Seminary, Carl George, author of *The Coming Church Revolution.* In this book, George presented a plan for building a super-church with the utilization of interdependent, interlocking, coalescing small groups. The concept of organization-building through such small groups is nothing new. As a matter of fact, in 1928 occultist H. G. Wells promoted such an organizational structure more than sixty years before Carl George penned his book:

> "The form of the conspiracy would not be a centralized organization but, rather, small groups of friends and coalitions of such groups." (This statement by H.G. Wells was quoted by Marilyn Ferguson in *The Aquarian Conspiracy.*) (21)

In addition to H.G. Wells and Marilyn Ferguson, The New Group of World Servers, a division of the Lucis Trust, chimes in with its own promotion of community through small groups:

> "...New age group work is, in reality, the outer manifestation of an inner and genuine spiritual condition... Buddha established his work in India through small group communities set up to be self-supporting and interdependent...Buddha saw this method as preparing for an eventual 'world community'...We have become interdependent in so many areas of human life, but not yet properly interrelated . Yet there is a common denominator—*relationship*." (22)

This quotation says it all. The working of the group-think philosophy is indeed a sign of a spiritual condition—not Godly, but spiritual. Just as Buddha stressed small groups and interdependence to build a "world community," the Lucis Trust realizes the success of such efforts is completely based on building relationships. Coincidentally (or not coincidentally), Dr. Warren stated, "*40 Days of Community is all about relationships.*" (23) After all, pragmatically speaking, if it worked for Buddha...

The group concept not only worked for Buddha, but also for Alice Bailey—the poet laureate of sorts for the Theosophical Society as well as the co-founder of the Lucis Trust. The Theosophical Society is a dark occult organization founded by Madam H.P. Blavatsky in the 19th Century. Her book, *The Secret Doctrine*, provided the roadmap for Adolf Hitler in his bid for an occult world empire. Alice Bailey, the once-removed successor to Blavatsky, was a prolific author of countless books dictated to her under automatic writing by her demon "spirit guide," Dwahl Kuhl. These books are used today by a division of the Lucis Trust, The Arcane School. The Arcane School supplies the writings of Alice Bailey as curriculum to those Freemasons chosen to advance into the occult hierarchy of that organization.

Alice Bailey's major doctrinal treatise is *The Externalization of the Hierarchy*. In this book, Bailey's demonic spirit guide established a doctrinal base for both "community" and group-think philosophies. However, the entire philosophy can be summarized with the following statement:

> "This must be a group work of a new order, wherein individual activity is subordinated to the group objective and the decision of the group in conclave...it is the will of the group... which is the point of major importance...*The final work of the Christ is to be framed in our identification to the whole.*" (24)

This quotation is doctrine from the very pit of Hell itself, and when Alice Bailey speaks of "the Christ," she does not speak of Jesus. Mrs. Bailey is speaking of Antichrist himself! Yet, a conservative, Southern Baptist preacher who is deemed one of the two most influential preachers in America today states:

> "You cannot be what God wants you to be by yourself...You cannot fulfill God's purposes for your life by yourself... I need a group!" (25)

Is not Dr. Warren's contention based on the same philosophical platform as that of the demonic spirit guide of Alice Bailey? Where is individual accountability to a Holy God? Where is the call to individual salvation?

Here's a news flash for those in the Church Growth Movement who would build a super church based on these group-think philosophies:

- McGavaran's Homogenous Unit Principle is not based on the Word of God, but on the behavioral sciences of modern psychology.
- The elevation of the group is a doctrine from Hell, and should not become the basis for church growth.
- The Word of God is clear that those lost individuals who stand before the Great White Throne Judgment will be judged as individuals. The sins of the father will not be ascribed to the son, nor will any group judgment determine eternal destiny.
- When a Christian stands before the Judgment Seat of Christ, he or she will stand there alone to receive or be denied reward. There will be no group therapy session to barter with Jesus for rewards or the lack thereof.

Biblical examples of the folly of the purpose-driven philosophy of *community* are prolific. Some examples include:

- God's call of Jeremiah
- God's direction to Elijah alone in a cave by a "still small voice."
- Elijah's time spent by the Brook Cherith
- The conversion of the Ethiopian Eunuch
- The command to "go into your closet" to pray and commune with God
- Even the example of Jesus, that He would go into the wilderness without the disciples to be alone with the Father.

The Bible is very clear that the Holy Spirit works in the heart of the *individual* who is attuned to His leading by hearing, studying, and meditating on His written Word. There is no group therapy session that can supersede the power and influence of the Almighty God as communicated through His inerrant Word.

BIBLE OR WITCHCRAFT?

In conclusion, the religious essence of the concept of community is best summarized by the witch, Starhawk:

> "The Goddess Religion is lived in community. Its primary focus is not individual salvation or enlightenment or enrichment but the growth and transformation that comes through intimate interactions and common struggles." (26)

The only difference in Starhawk's doctrine and teaching of *40 Days of Community* is the fact that the leaders of the 40 Days program contend that focusing on the group will *result* in individual salvation. However, one must seriously question even the validity of professions that result from methods that are steeped in New Age, occult, and even demonic methodologies.

ENDNOTES

(1) Warren, Rick. "40 Days of Community," Saddleback Community Church, Audio Disc, September- November, 2004.

(2) Starhawk. *The Spiral Dance*, Harper Publishing, San Francisco, 1979, p.22.

(3) Ephesian 1:22-23.

(4) Ephesians 2:19-22.

(5) Warren.

(6) Ibid.

(7) I Corinthians 2:18.

(8) Hebrews 4:12.

(9) Starhawk.

(10) "Where Wild Things Live: Men Embracing the Shadow and the Sacred," The Rowe Camp—1995.

(11) Wallace-Murphy, Tim. *Cracking the Symbol Code*, Watkins Publishing, London, 2005, p.138.

(12) *The Declaration of Interdependence*. Earth Summit, Rio de Janeiro, 1992.

(13) Cuddy, D.L. *A Chronological History of the New World Order*, www.constitution.org/col/cuddy_nwo.htm.

(14) Ibid.

(15) Warren.

(16) Ferguson, Marilyn. *The Aquarian Conspiracy*, J.P. Tarcher, Inc., Los Angeles, CA., 1980, p.402.

(17) Ibid. p.402.

(18) Ibid. p.369.

(19) Ibid. p.411.

(20) Ibid. p. 406.

(21) Wells, H.G. As quoted by Marilyn Ferguson, *The Aquarian Conspiracy*, p.213.

(22) Bailey, Mary. *A Learning Experience*, Lucis Trust, New York, 1990, pp. 96-97.

(23) Warren

(24) Bailey, Alice. *Externalization of the Hierarchy*, Lucis Publishing, New York, 1957, pp. 324,413.

(25) Warren.

(26) Starhawk.

Chapter 4

Building Heaven on Earth

"Perhaps the most dangerous notion of all is the belief that given the proper amount of power and the ability to manipulate and manage, well-intentioned men can create heaven on earth." (1)

THE GLOBAL COMMUNITY

Since the time of the Tower of Babel, men have sought the establishment of an all-encompassing world government that would bind all of mankind into one interdependent human community. A very casual study of secular history is witness to this very fact, as world empires have risen and fallen riding the crest of the waves that swept across the massive sands of all of humanity. These world empires were exemplified in the Assyrian Empire, the Egyptian Empire, the Babylonian Empire, the Medo-Persian Empire, the Grecian Empire, and finally the Roman Empire. Additionally, there were other individuals who died trying to emulate the likes of the Pharaohs, Sennacherib, Nebuchadnezzar, Darius, Alexander, and the Caesars. Their names are generally not connected to acts of great benevolence, but they do cover quite a few pages in the History of Civilization textbooks.

These names include such individuals as Napoleon Bonaparte, Genghis Khan, and Adolf Hitler. If history has not characterized these particular individuals in exactly the noblest manner, there was also the United Kingdom of Great Britain with "noble," imperialistic tentacles that spread across the face of the earth well into the Twentieth Century. However, there is one factor that most tend to ignore when embarking on a study of world empires, and this very factor states that any *human world government* (whether benevolent or tyrannical) is in diametric opposition to the plan of God for mankind. Furthermore, those who study the Word of God recognize that the next world empire will be the most "evil" of all "evil empires," ruled by Antichrist himself.

A careful reading of the account of the Tower of Babel in Genesis 11 reveals the true purpose of the scattering of the citizens of Babel across the face of the earth. The *Bible* records that God scattered mankind in order to keep them from doing whatever they could imagine. Before questioning God's motives in so adamantly suppressing freedom of expression, one must exercise the first rule of biblical interpretation: "*Always let Scripture interpret other Scripture.*" For just two chapters earlier, in Genesis 8:21, God confirmed to Noah after the Flood, "... *the imagination of man's heart is evil from his youth.*" Now if the imagination of the heart of man is innately evil as God states in Genesis 8, any one-world system comprised of all humanity will inevitably pool all of the evil resources that humanity can imagine to serve Lucifer---not God. Therefore, God scattered the inhabitants who dwelled on the Plains of Shinar by confusing their languages. This action by God also created the foundation of the nation-state—obviously God's geo-political plan for the inhabitants of Planet Earth.

The second danger imposed by the "evil imagination" of mankind is that of a one-world religion. This is evidenced by the fact that each of the afore-mentioned world empires (as well as many other subsequent, less expansive kingdoms) also imposed a "state religion." Additionally, the Bible teaches that the final world empire of Antichrist will also boast a single world religion—the worship of the "Dragon who gave power to the Beast." (2) Therefore, if "well-intentioned men" as Barry Goldwater labeled them, are striving to build their "heaven on earth," "New Atlantis," or "New World Order;" these plans will by default not only be based on political aspirations that oppose the plan of God, but also must unite all religions into an all-encompassing worship of Lucifer himself.

GLOBAL COMMUNITY= KINGDOM OF ANTICHRIST

When one then "takes off his or her blinders" and views history from the perspective that current events are locked on a course that will indeed produce this Luciferic Kingdom, that individual will begin to see current political and religious events in an entirely different light. However, the opposite is also true. If one misinterprets or violates the context of Word of God to the extent of envisioning the current course of history to produce the "Kingdom of God," then that individual may well fall into the trap of misinterpreting and/or supporting the very factors that will contribute to the prerequisite Luciferic Kingdom of Antichrist.

In way of clarification, the Millennial Kingdom of God ruled by none other than Jesus Christ will most assuredly become a reality. Jesus Himself will return to the earth with the redeemed saints and defeat Antichrist. He will also bind Lucifer in the "bottomless pit" for a period of 1000 literal years—thus the designation of "Millennial Kingdom." This action will force the fall of the "New World Order," and will then initiate the reign of Jesus on the earth in fulfillment of His promises to the patriarchs of Israel and to His servant, David. Though the raptured and glorified Church will be very involved in this kingdom, the Millennial Kingdom will not be "built" until the Second Coming of Christ.

If then God's judgment will fall upon the earth to the extent that two-thirds of the land mass of the planet will be devastated and the entire population of unbelieving mankind annihilated; (3) why should the saved of this present age even imagine that they can help God build His earthly kingdom? According to the Word of God, the earthly Kingdom of God will not appear until after the earth is devastated. Additionally, not only will God certainly not need any human help to build His earthly kingdom; but the construction will be well above and beyond human capabilities.

Therefore, the "Kingdom" terminology currently thrown around by high profile evangelicals is totally out of context with the teachings of the Word of God. Yes, all Christians are members of or "children of" the "Kingdom of Heaven," but this is the kingdom of which Jesus spoke when He declared to Pilate, "My kingdom is not of this world." (4) Furthermore, when an individual is born again of the Holy Spirit of God, that individual does indeed become a part of, and in one respect increases the size of the "Kingdom of Heaven." However, the saved of the earth in this present Age of Grace are in no way, shape, or form building an earthly "Kingdom of God" that will manifest itself as a geo-political entity, and to designate their actions as such is playing with fire. Distressingly, so many Christians have no clue as to exactly how hot the fire of Hell can become if one gets too close.

THE LONG WAR AGAINST GOD

In his book, *The Long War Against God*, Dr. Henry Morris laid out the plan of Lucifer to overthrow God. He further gave evidences that Lucifer truly believes he can defeat God, and he realizes his time is getting short. In agreement with this premise, as the "End of Days" draws closer, Lucifer is turning up the heat to reach his final objective. It is the fire generated from the heat of battle that will burn those who stray too far from the truth of the Word of God. Thus, to truly fight on the Lord's side and "contend for the Faith," one must surely understand the goals and tactics of the enemy.

A study of history literally reveals that Luciferic forces have one major goal—the establishment of the Kingdom of Antichrist. The fruition of this goal, even now after some 4400 years of the strategic planning, has obviously not transpired overnight. This is clearly illustrated by the example of Western society, where the influence of Christianity for the first 1750 years from the establishment of the Church instilled attitudes and values among broad-based western society more consistent with the teachings of Scripture than pre-Christian pagan values. However, winds of change have been blowing for several centuries, and the subtle, strategic transition is gradually making itself manifest.

This manifest transition of a change in attitudes and values has not come to pass in a violent, catastrophic, ravaging, or societal-altering cataclysm. Rather, the changes have been instigated subtly, slowly, systematically, and intentionally. At the risk of excessive historical over-analysis, one must at a minimum examine the goals and aspirations of those involved directly with Luciferian forces to reach a thorough understanding of the desire not only for a new political paradigm, but also for a "New Paradigm Church" that will fall into the arms of Antichrist without so much as a whisper of protest.

A NEW WORLD ORDER

Initially, one must understand that the call for this new political/religious paradigm known as the "New World Order" is based primarily on the ancient values of those who lived in the third generation after the Flood of Noah and their demonically instigated desire for a return to the ungodly civilization that existed prior to the Flood. As has been implied earlier in this manuscript, Nimrod honestly attempted to open the gate for demonic control of all of mankind; but even with Lucifer's defeat at the

Tower of Babel, world empires rose and flourished until the 5th Century AD.

Even prior to this point in history, the so-called great sages and wise men who embraced the occult mysteries began to prophecy of a "golden age" that would restore the earth to a state of paradise. These mysteries were then held in store by secret societies of occult initiates, Kabbalists, Gnostics or even "Gnostic Christians." All of this secret knowledge was converted to definitive action in the 16th Century work of Sir Francis Bacon when he penned his allegory, *The New Atlantis*. Even more significantly, Bacon and his accomplices presented a step-by-step plan for the restoration of a state of paradise upon earth. (5)

Bacon enabled the theories behind *The New Atlantis* to be put into practical application with the colonization of the New World. It was within this climate that the struggle between those who would build a utopian heaven on earth and those who would found a nation based on the principles of the Word of God not only escalated to new heights, but made the United States of America the major battleground in the preservation of the truth.

By the 20th Century, occult forces world wide began to make bold initiatives. In her book, *The Externalization of the Hierarchy*, occultist Alice Bailey (via automatic writing) recorded the words of her spirit guide (demon) Djwahl Kuhl:

> "1934 marks the beginning of the organizing of the men and women... the group work of a new order...(with) progress defined by service... the work of the Brotherhood ... the Forces of Light... (and) out of the spoliation of all existing culture and civilization, the new world order must be built." (6)

These same concepts were parroted by Fabian Socialist and noted author, HG Wells:

> "The organization of this that I call the Open Conspiracy... which will ultimately supply teaching, coercive and directive public services to the whole world, is the

immediate task before all rational people... a planned world-state is appearing at a thousand points.... a 'collectivist one-world state' or 'new world order' comprised of 'socialist democracies'....nationalist individualism...is the world's disease...The manifest necessity for some collective world control to eliminate warfare and ...necessity for a collective control of the economic and biological life of mankind, are aspects of one and the same process." I propose that this be accomplished through 'universal law' and propaganda (or education)." (7)

One realizes the danger involved when the leaders of the public education system chime into the occult scenario:

> "The Progressive Education Association, organized by John Dewey (the infamous Father of Progressive Education), in 1947 addressed the teachers of the nation, calling for 'the establishment of a genuine world order'... an order in which national sovereignty is subordinate to the world authority... an order in which 'world citizenship' thus assumes at last equal status with national citizenship.... As the old order is crumbling, and there is a new and free order struggling to be born... There is a fever of nationalism... (but) the nation-state is becoming less and less competent to perform its international political tasks.... These are some of the reasons pressing us to lead vigorously toward the true building of a new world order..." (8)

The essence of this sentiment aroused suspicion even in the Congress of the United States. On April 24, 1954, Rep. Usher Burdick, Republican of Nebraska related to Congress:

> "Mr.Speaker, there can be no doubt that there now exists widespread understanding and agreement made between the agents of this Government and the United Nations and North Atlantic Treaty Organization to build a world government, and to make the United States a part of it--regardless of our Constitution, laws, and traditions...This is to be done in the name of peace...but will result in the total

> destruction of our liberty. The agents representing the United States may not be deliberately trying to do this treasonable work, but the best that can be said for them is that they are dupes…" (9)

By the 1970s, things had grown progressively worse. Richard Gardner wrote in *Foreign Affairs,* the official publication of the Council for Foreign Relations:

> "In short, the 'house of world order' will have to be built from the bottom up rather than from the top down...an end run around national sovereignty, eroding it piece by piece, will accomplish much more than the old-fashioned frontal assault…" (10)

In 1975, the United States Legislature: 32 Senators and 92 Representatives signed the "Declaration of Interdependence" discussed earlier in this manuscript. This document stated:

> "…we must join with others to bring forth a new world order.... Narrow notions of national sovereignty must not be permitted to curtail that obligation." (11)

Once the Clinton Administration controlled the Washington bureaucracy, a deteriorating situation became even more blatant. Under Secretary of State, Strobe Talbot, a member of the World Federalists, made this alarming statement:

> "In the next century, nations as we know it will be obsolete; all states will recognize a single, global authority. Maybe national sovereignty wasn't such a great idea after all." (12)

Even though statements such as those made by Talbot are in essence predicting the appearance of the kingdom of Antichrist, the phrase "new world order" is generally construed by the average American as a term used by right wing fanatics who live in a constant and overwhelming fog of incurable, and ultimately fatal paranoia. However, the facts prove quite to the contrary. The use of this terminology by the afore-mentioned particular individuals (in their own words) verifies that there truly exists an occultist hierarchy that is, in fact, endeavoring to build a utopian socialist society based on the antediluvian mysteries of Luciferic origin.

To accuse these individuals of deliberately practicing the religion of Satanism may well be somewhat extreme, but to identify their motivations as Luciferian inspiration is certainly anything but extreme. For the attacks on national sovereignty exhibited in the preceding quotations are, in reality, attacks on the plan of Almighty God. Even though all those who make such attacks may not overtly pledge allegiance to Lucifer, they are certainly promoting the Luciferian agenda---even if such promotion is done through ignorance.

COMMON VALUES: BUILDING BLOCKS OF GLOBALISM

As illustrated in Chapter 2, if evil always appeared as evil, the enticement to evil works would not be as easily "sold" to an unsuspecting population. However, if the plan of Lucifer was "sold" as a plan to develop a human community by establishing unity in diversity, how much more successful could this plan become? Furthermore, if one were aspire to create globalistic unity in diversity, what strategy would serve to unify those of diverse backgrounds, religions, and cultures?

The solution to this question is really quite simple (the implementation of the solution is not so simple, but the solution itself is very simple): *seek common ground among the diverse and cultivate it.* Once common ground is found, build upon this common ground with a system of common values, and thus establish unity. Once common values are established, those whose values are in opposition to the majority must be changed (or else).

The heart of the issue revolves around the fact *that globalistic, one-world values are in direct conflict with those of not only the fundamental concepts of true Christianity, but also with the attitudes and values of those who made this country great.* For example, the basic values of those that forged a nation in the "new world" from the wilderness were based on rugged individualism that exemplified the "pioneer spirit" of these individuals. In a similar fashion, the Christian faith is also based on individual salvation and an individual's accountability to and relationship with Almighty God.

In contrast, *the values of the "new paradigm" must emphasize the good of the group*—not the individual, and it is this enshrinement of the group parroted by occult organizations and other globalists that has infiltrated the psyche of recent generations. It is this same group-think value system that has subtly steamrolled the Church of Jesus Christ, and most of its members do not even realize what has happened. There are those that are starting to ask the question, "How did this happen?" However, most have been duped into changing their attitudes to the point that they are at (or have plunged over) the precipice of embracing postmodern tolerance and dismissing the eternal truths of the Word of God.

While the move for a change in values is outwardly political, it will ultimately result in sweeping spiritual changes. The political aspect has been openly voiced on several fronts. The United Nations publication, *Our Global Neighborhood*, makes plea after plea for new values that stress the need create a new global ethic:

> "The new world order must be organized around the notion of governance of diversity, not uniformity; governance of democracy, not dominion.... *built on the foundation of an ascendancy of global neighborhood values over divisive nationalism..."* (13)

Former Russian Premier, Mikhail Gorbachev, speaking as the founder of the radical environmental group, Green Cross, stated:

> "Today humankind is facing a choice...we need to find a new paradigm ...that can be based on the common values...developed over many centuries...the search for a new paradigm should be a search for synthesis, for what is common and unites people, countries, and nations, rather than what divides them." (14)

Note that the "new paradigm" of which he speaks once again voices the Hegelian Dialectical process in exactly the same manner as voiced by HG Wells: the search for synthesis—the common ground that unites the group—and thus all of mankind. This again is the same plan as attempted by Nimrod—the plan that Almighty God rejected. Mankind, under the direct influence and direction of Lucifer is seeking to worship and serve the creature over the Creator by rebuilding the Tower of Babel-- the precious New World Order.

Other organizations are touting the same strategy. For example, the Earth Charter, directed by Dr. Stephen Rockefeller, states:

> "...a statement of fundamental principles...clarifying humanities shared values and developing a new global ethic for a sustainable way of life.... Earth stands at a defining moment..dramatic rise in population...dominate pattern of production and consumption...degrading environment.... massive extinction of species... poverty ...crime...violence...Fundamental changes in our attitudes, values, and ways of living...we recognize the urgent need for a shared vision of basic values that will provide an ethical foundation for the emerging world community...we affirm the following principles for sustainable development..." (15)

Once again, in the Earth Charter there appears the group-think values system. A values system that will diminish the importance of the individual, personal liberties, and personal accountability to an Almighty God—it is all about the group. The thesis of the Earth Charter is that humanity must change its values or face both destruction of the earth and extinction of the human species. As Wells stated, humanity must move forward into the Aquarian Age—the age when man realizes that he, in fact, is God.

At stake here is a major religious issue, for this movement is religious as well as a political. This fact is clearly evidenced on many fronts. As *Our Global Neighborhood* declares:

> "We need a set of common, core values around which we can unite people, irrespective of their cultural, political, *religious*... backgrounds." (16)

However, if you are to unite mankind based on common religious values, what religion will the world embrace? World Goodwill, a division of Lucis Trust states:

> "...Preparation by men and women of goodwill is needed to introduce *new values* for living, new standards of behavior, new attitudes...of *non-separateness and cooperation* leading to right human relations and a world at peace. The coming World Teacher will be mainly concerned with the requirements for a *new world order*... (17)
>
> ...The New Group of World Servers...can be regarded as the embodiment of the *emerging Kingdom of God on earth*, but it should be remembered that this kingdom is not a Christian kingdom or an earthly government" (18)

Lucis Trust and the New Group of World Servers are without question working in preparation for the coming of the world ruler—none other than Antichrist. Furthermore, their terminology should make any discerning Christian take note of all who openly have issued the call for the New World Order or those who are seeking to "build 'the Kingdom of God.'" These are the individuals who are in zombie-like fashion marching to the drumbeat of Lucifer and preparing the earth for Antichrist himself.

Therefore, the efforts to build "heaven on earth" via a global community are working for a cause that will lead to the earthly Kingdom of Antichrist. For the Scripture is very clear that the consummate "evil empire" will arise at the end of this current age, and it will be through this sequence of events that God will not only pour out His wrath upon sinful man, but He will again deal with Israel in order to secure the remnant that will be saved to inhabit the Millennial Kingdom of Jesus Christ.

REPLACEMENT & KINGDOM THEOLOGY

Now that the reader understands the nature of the "fire" with which high profile evangelicals are playing, a determination must be made of not only how this "fire" started, but where it is spreading, and exactly what or who is fueling the flames. In review, and in a nutshell, the theological problems that result from a perversion of Scripture whereby error is compounded on error have their origin in the early centuries of the Church.

The early church faced the attacks of Lucifer on many fronts, and these attacks can be easily consigned to two categories—external and internal. The external attacks came from the likes of the Jewish authorities that crucified Christ and later the empirical rulers of the Roman Empire. Though there were many martyrs in the early Church, external persecution only fueled the flames of evangelism, and the Church continued to grow at a phenomenal rate.

The internal attacks, however, were far more damaging on a long term basis. These attacks came from those "Church Fathers" who embraced the heresies of Aryanism, Gnosticism, and Manichaeism to name just a few. It was the infiltration of these philosophies that prompted the authors of the New Testament under the direction of the Holy Spirit to sound the warning of false teachers who "crept in unawares." Furthermore, it was in response to these blatant attacks on primarily the person and deity of Jesus Christ that initiated the call for the Council of Nicea. This council, called by Emperor Constantine, and subsequent councils became the primary vehicles in the formation of the Roman Catholic machine. It was this very institution that garnished the falling pieces of a crumbling empire to build an organization with a "form of godliness," but was in reality as Jesus described the Pharisees of His time—"whited sepulchres full of dead mens' bones." (19)

It was the Roman Catholic Church that conceived the unbiblical notions of "Replacement Theology" and the Church as the earthly "Kingdom of God." Though these are two distinct doctrines, they go hand-in-hand to form an eschatology that violates the contextual interpretation of the Word of God. Simply stated, the two teachings are as follows:

- Replacement Theology—This doctrine teaches that because the nation of Israel rejected and crucified Christ, God rejected Israel as His chosen people. Furthermore, not only has God now rejected Israel, the Church has replaced Israel as "God's chosen people."

Subsequently, all Old Testament promises made to Israel have now been passed to the Church; and since God has rejected Israel, the Jewish people have become the dregs of society, lower life forms than human beings, and are to be punished for the actions of their forefathers' rejection of Jesus as their Messiah.

- Kingdom of God—As a result of God's rejection of Israel and the Church's new inheritance of Old Testament promises, the prophesied "Kingdom" is now manifested in the Church. In other words, according to this teaching the 1000 year reign of Christ is not a literal prophecy but is only an allegory describing the Church. The Church then is the Kingdom of God on Earth, and will reign over the affairs of men as God's representatives until Jesus returns to "make all things new." The logical conclusion of this chain of reasoning dictates that in spite of all the flagrant evil witnessed in modern society, this is the Millennium.

These two doctrines have become more dangerous as the years have progressed. This is primarily due to the incomplete obedience of the reformers of the Protestant Reformation. The Protestant Reformation was godly in many of its aspects. However, the reformers failed to follow the doctrine of Scriptural Separation. They chose to attempt to reform the evil ways of the papacy rather than separate from it. They were forced into separation when the Roman Church excommunicated them, but that was never their intention. As a result, many of the erroneous doctrines of Catholicism filtered into the true Protestant churches—Lutheran and Presbyterian. (Baptists, Methodists, Anglicans, and Episcopalians though generally grouped into the Protestant genre, were not formed as a direct result of the Protestant Reformation.) Among the erroneous doctrines that transferred from Catholicism were Infant Baptism, Replacement Theology, and Post-Millennial Eschatology. The Presbyterian connection to Calvin's Covenant Theology became the primary catalyst for doctrinal error to the modern Evangelical movement.

REFORMING FUNDAMENTALISM

The Twentieth Century began with great spiritual upheavals. The religious skepticism that began in the mid-Nineteenth Century in Great

Britain grew to maturity in the late 1920s. With the uproar that resulted from the Scopes Monkey Trial, Skepticism moved up (or down, depending on your perspective) a notch to full-fledged Modernism. The Modernist (among other erroneous teachings) denied the Inspiration and Inerrancy of Scripture, the Virgin Birth of Christ, the Blood Atonement of Christ's vicarious death, and Jesus' Bodily Resurrection from the tomb. Modernism quickly infiltrated the agencies and universities of the Mainline Protestant organizations, and as a result, the "Long War Against God" was elevated to new levels.

It was the backlash of these events that led to the coining of the term "Fundamentalist," and Christian Fundamentalism became the safe harbor for those who not only stood for the doctrines that the Modernists denied, but were willing to militantly defend those doctrines and separate themselves from those who denied the Faith. The Fundamentalist movement in the United States followed the example Charles Spurgeon in Nineteenth Century Britain, and was led by the likes of Tozer, Schofield, Gordon, Ironside, Jones, Rice, McIntire, and Machen. These men carried the torch for the cause of Christ through tumultuous times, and only eternity will reveal the true fruits of their labors.

However, there were those who were offended by the "backwoods" style of the Fundamentalists, and led by a conservative Presbyterian minister, Dr. Harold Ockenga, a new movement was formed. Those who led this movement felt that the Fundamentalists failed to add a "social philosophy" with the message of salvation. They also accused Fundamentalists of delving too much into personalities that embraced error. These "New Evangelicals," as they called themselves, approached modern issues from the perspective that scientific questions such as the "Flood," the age of the earth, and creation should be left to the intellectuals (This, in essence, was an attack on the intellect of Fundamentalist leaders). Most significantly, however, was the contention that Christians should not *separate from* apostasy (as the Bible teaches), but rather, true Christians should *infiltrate* apostate churches and organizations to attempt conversion. The New Evangelicals formed their own seminary to promote their ideas, and the graduates of Fuller Theological Seminary are now the leaders in the "New Paradigm Church."

The establishment of the New Evangelical philosophy was promoted on a global level by its first "poster-child," Dr. Billy Graham, and the movement that began as a ripple within true Christianity began to slowly swell to the tidal wave it has become today. The movement today is led by the heir-apparent to Dr. Graham, Fuller Seminary graduate, Dr. Rick Warren. Dr. Warren himself stated that he is leading a "New Reformation" with his outcome-based approach to ministry, and he is absolutely correct. However, what he does not tell you is that this "New Reformation" began in 1948 when Harold Ockenga, Charles Fuller, and others who formed the National Association of Evangelicals conceived the "New Evangelical" philosophy in order to reform Fundamentalism.

BACK TO THE GLOBAL COMMUNITY

At this point, one may ask, "So how does Rick Warren, the NAE, Billy Graham, and Replacement Theology correlate to globalism, "heaven on earth," or building an interdependent human community?" That is an excellent question, and it deserves a good answer. The answer lies in the identification of the individual that served as the conduit between the promoters of a utopian society and the Evangelical Church—one Peter Drucker.

DRUCKER, SYSTEMS THEORY, & UTOPIA

Peter Drucker, the infamous business management guru who passed away in November of 2005, became very popular in Evangelical circles in the 1990s. Drucker's claim to fame was staked to the rebuilding of the post-World War II Japanese economy, and his management system, *Management by Objective*, is an outcome-based system that emphasizes a syllogistic process to achieve a pre-determined outcome.

Peter Drucker's interface with the Church came primarily from the efforts of Texas TV magnet, Bob Buford. Buford, the author of the best-selling book, *Halftime*, was president of the Peter Drucker Foundation, an organization that later became *The Leadership Network*. Through these organizations, Buford and Drucker worked with large mega-churches (including Saddleback Community Church and Rick Warren) to develop organizational structures to insure further growth and stability.

Drucker's interest in these projects was very significant, as he spent the last half of his life working with churches and other nonprofit organizations to develop what he called "community" in order to "save society from despair." (20) His concept of "community" is based on the complete collaboration of what he called the "the three pillars of society"—the State, the Corporation, and Non-profits. It would be, according to Drucker, the bonding of these three "pillars" that a world "community" could reasonably be formed. He called this model the "3-Legged Stool," with the three pillars supporting the top of the concept—"Community." According to *Christianity Today*, Drucker saw this "community" as did John Dewey: "a new form of society struggling to get out of its chrysalis." Drucker, however, conceived this new societal breakout "with churches and nonprofits leading the way." (21)

This model for world community is nothing new. It is the basic "systems approach" of the "new world order" that has been long parroted by occult and globalist sources for more than a century. In his 1973 book, *With No Apologies,* Barry Goldwater conveyed that the blatantly globalist Trilateral Commission sought to build their "heaven on earth" by seizing the "4 Corners of Power"—Political, Economic, Religious, and Educational. (22) By combining The Trilateralist "Educational" and "Religious" subsystems into "Non-profits," one sees the identical structure as illustrated by Drucker's "3-legged stool." Even as early as the 19th Century, the infamous occultist, Alexandre Saint Yves d'Alveydre, spoke of the control of the "3 pillars of society:" religious, financial, and political to advance his theories of Synarchy, government by secret societies. (23) The pillars of St. Yves are the same as those of Drucker when you include religion as the dominant component of Drucker's "Non-profits," and they both equate to the plan of the Trilateral Commission.

Thus, no one should be too surprised that Drucker spent the last half of his life working to bring the non-profit leg into the fold—for until the 1970s, the growth of Christian Fundamentalism posed the greatest threat on earth to Drucker's utopian community. For with the rapid growth of evangelical and fundamentalist Christianity in the US (as late as the early 1970s, Independent Baptist churches were the fastest growing churches in the world), utopian systems planners were tasked with the necessity of amalgamating this growing segment of society into the "system" because it had grown to large to be controlled any longer outside of the system. In a nutshell, the Bible-believing Christian Fundamentalists and Evangelical Christians were standing in the middle of the "yellow brick road," Bible in hand, and blocking the route to Oz. Someone then needed to step forward and develop a plan to turn these rebels into allies that would joyously join Dorothy, the Tin Man, and the Cowardly Lion in skipping hand-in-hand down the "yellow brick road" to the fair utopia of Oz. The question was then, simply stated: "How could this be accomplished?"

In the late 1960s and early 1970s the Modernist denominations, though they were an integral part of the "system," were in rapid decline. The "New Evangelicals" led by the NAE and their poster child, Dr. Billy Graham, had little or no influence on those in the swelling Fundamentalist camp. As a matter of fact, Dr. Graham and the NAE were openly scorned by the surging Independent Baptists, the American Council of Christian Churches, the International Council of Christian Churches, and other Fundamentalist groups. So how could a plan be developed to slow down and turn around these "fanatics?"

In 1973, the essence of the plan was laid out in Richard Gardner's article in the magazine of the Council for Foreign Relations, *Foreign Affairs*. The article entitled "The Hard Road to World Order," previously quoted in this chapter stated:

> "In short, the 'house of world order' will have to be built from the bottom up rather than from the top down...an end run around national sovereignty, eroding it piece by piece, will accomplish much more than the old-fashioned frontal assault..." (24)

Though this particular quotation specifically mentioned national sovereignty as the perceived villain, the principle also applied to right wing Christian Fundamentalists and Evangelicals. In essence, such a plan would be one of infiltration and covert manipulation to first slow down and finally neutralize any resistance to a utopian globalist system by those who called themselves Bible-believing Christians. The infiltration (even if those who were the leaders were well-intentioned dupes and patsies) actually began with the philosophies of Ockenga, McGavaran, and Fuller

Seminary. Its propaganda was published in *Christianity Today* and championed by Dr. Billy Graham. There are even some who contend that globalist covert operations were responsible for "Second Wave" of the Charismatic Movement of the late 1970s. (25) All of this was the operational process of Gardner's proposal of "piecemeal functionalism" that would institute a "paradigm shift" in baby steps, piece-by piece, and bringing the water to such a slow boil that the frog would never know he was going to be served up like chopped liver.

By the 1990s change was in the air. The Charismatic Movement propelled the Assembles of God to replace the Fundamentalist Independent Baptists as the fastest growing churches in the world. However, the transition was not complete. Dr. Graham was getting old, and a new replacement needed to be found.

40 DAYS OF PEACE, & THE GLOBAL P.E.A.C.E. PLAN

Enter Dr. Rick Warren. Warren, a Fuller Seminary graduate and pastor of Saddleback Community Church, had become a close friend of Peter Drucker. He entertained Drucker in his home, and stated that he read everything Drucker had written. Drucker called Dr. Warren the "inventor of perpetual revival." (26) With the publishing of *The Purpose-Driven Church* and *The Purpose –Driven Life*, Warren has become known as "America's Pastor," and has since become the heir apparent to the legacy of Dr. Billy Graham. His "community," "Global Christian," and "new paradigm" terminology echo not only the teachings of the utopian Drucker, but also occultist such as Alice Bailey and Marilyn Ferguson. Additionally, his "seeker-sensitive" approach to ministry fully incorporates the "third way" occult principle of knowledge without doctrine. (27)

Much has been detailed in this manuscript of the philosophies and problems with *The Purpose-Driven Life* and Dr. Warren's program of *40 Days of Community*, but in the autumn of 2005, Saddleback Community Church kicked off Dr. Warren's most ambitious program to date, *40 Days of Peace*. The *40 Days of Peace* program officially introduced Dr. Warren's "P.E.A.C.E. Plan," whereby churches all over the world would address what Warren calls the "five biggest problems" that face mankind: Spiritual Emptiness, Lack of Education, Poverty, Disease, and Lack of

Effective Leadership. (28) It is not the intention of the author in this venue to present a point by point critique the P.E.A.C.E. Plan. As a matter of fact, as social programs go, this author is in agreement with and commends many of the methods and philosophies exercised within a plan that takes a new, logical, innovative approach in areas where governmental social programs have miserably failed in reducing poverty, illiteracy, and disease. (Frankly, the "leadership" issue is a completely different subject, and will be discussed at length in the next chapter.)

However, from a religious perspective, there is also much of the underlying concept of this plan that is very distressing. The following is a brief analysis of these concerns:

Is a program such as the P.E.A.C.E. plan really the mission of the Church?

The fact of the matter is that Dr. Rick Warren is fulfilling the 1948 vision conceived by Dr. Harold Ockenga in his criticism of Fundamentalism. Dr. Ockenga felt that there should be a balance between preaching a Modernist social gospel and the strict adherence of Fundamentalists to concentrate primarily on the spiritual condition of the individual. Of the four core concepts of the "New Evangelism," number 1 on the list is as follows:

> *"New Evangelicals would address the social issues that Fundamentalists avoided. New Evangelicals would include with salvation a 'social philosophy.'"* (29)

There is no question that the Church has lost focus of its primary mission. That mission is 2-fold: *Evangelization and Edification*. The Church is to lead others to the saving knowledge of Jesus Christ and train those individuals to live their lives in accordance to the principles of the Word of God. It is that simple. Dr. Rick Warren would agree with that statement, and would probably defend the P.E.A.C.E. Plan as a means to that end. However, there are two problems with such a contention. 1) Does the Holy Spirit of God speak to the hearts of individuals through the fulfillment of felt needs or through His Word? 2) Will the concentration of meeting felt needs make the preaching of the Word of God a secondary priority to jobs, houses, education, etc.?

Now there is no question that great missionaries who won many to Christ were (or are) medical doctors, pilots, and school teachers. However, an entire program that concentrates on felt needs is more likely to end up as the ministry of Mother Teresa, who stated that in her ministry, there was no dealing with the spiritual condition of those who were Hindu or Buddhist; but rather, they concentrated on doing all they could to comfort and encourage them in their physical maladies.

Also, it is not the contention of this author that Fundamentalists have always upheld the primary mission of the church. For in spite of the contentions of some high-profile Fundamentalists of the past, the mission of the Church has never been to fight Communism or promote patriotism. These issues along with others have been used as marketing methods to reach individuals; but more often than not, the marketing methods surpass the mission it seeks to accomplish. If the P.E.A.C.E. Plan would win the lost to Christ and then seek to meet the needs of those individuals, that portion of the plan would be completely biblical. However, the P.E.A.C.E. Plan as it has been presented is a cart-before-the-horse social program that emphasizes felt needs over the spiritual condition of lost souls.

Will the implementation of such a plan utilizing dialectical small groups deter the saving work of the Holy Spirit?

Chapter 13 of this author's previous book, *Outcome-based Religion: Purpose, Apostasy, and the New Paradigm Church* dealt with the dialectical process of group dynamics that can potentially destroy the faith of those in "churches" whose foundation is based in small groups. Dr. Warren stated that the goal of the P.E.A.C.E. Plan is to build thousands of churches world-wide on the small group, metachurch plan. If this purpose-driven, outcome-based, systems-based philosophy is multiplied around the world through this P.E.A.C.E. Plan, it could be the most devastating blow to true Christianity ever witnessed. For this philosophy is a recipe for a disastrous paradigm shift away from the teachings of the cardinal doctrines of the Word of God to a new hybrid religion that may well meet the felt needs of those involved while condemning their souls for eternity.

Will the execution of a global social program lead to the promotion of other globalist agendas?

Unfortunately, this question has already been answered. *The New York Times* reported on February 8, 2006 that 86 evangelical Christian leaders decided to climb on the band wagon with radical environmentalists by joining the Evangelical Climate Initiative to fight Global Warming. Among the signers of this initiative were Rick Warren and Leith Anderson, two of the primary leaders of the Church Growth Movement. (Anderson is now the interim president of the National Association of Evangelicals,. replacing the disgraced Ted Haggard.) Not only does this align them with individuals such as Mikhail Gorbechev (quoted earlier in this chapter) whose religion is that of the worship of Gaia or Mother Earth, but this initiative is also funded by globalists organizations such as the Rockefeller Foundation and the Pew Charitable Trust. (30)

Let's ask these "great Christian leaders" a few basic questions on biblical eschatology: Do you believe that the Millennium is a literal prophecy, and Jesus will reign over the earth? If you answer that question "yes," how can you support an initiative whose basic premise is that man is going to destroy the earth and make it uninhabitable? Further, how can you align yourselves with those who believe that the earth is a living entity, a personification of the Mother Goddess, and use the "global environmental agenda" as an evangelization platform for a false pagan religion? What is your agenda behind joining a pagan, globalist initiative?

Actually, even without receiving an answer to these questions, the die has been cast on these individuals. There must be deeper issues lurking behind the facade of outward "Christian" leadership. The essence of these issues can truly be discovered when one delves into the theology taught (or not taught) from the pulpits of the new paradigm churches.

THE GLOBAL PEACE PLAN & THE KINGDOM OF GOD

In the final installment of his *40 Days of Peace* at Saddleback Church in November of 2005, Dr. Rick Warren gave the reasons why he and his followers are going to implement the Global P.E.A.C.E. Plan. He listed several reasons as to why they would take on such a bold plan, but his final point told the entire story. He stated this point as "The Inevitability of History."

Dr. Warren stated that while the P.E.A.C.E. Plan is a large undertaking, God has a bigger plan. God's big plan is the Kingdom of God on earth, *and the P.E.A.C.E. plan will become one more step toward fulfilling God's ultimate goal.* Now the very thesis of this chapter has been established to prove that Christians in this Age of Grace *will not build the Kingdom of God* on earth due to the fact that the Luciferic New World Order will be the next world kingdom. Furthermore, Bible prophecy is succinctly clear that this Kingdom of Antichrist will be based on deception. (See II Thessalonians 2) Therefore, the danger here is clearly illustrated by those "conservative Christians" who have joined hands with utopian social planners such as the late Peter Drucker to initiate this "new reformation" of "learning without doctrine."

To that end, one must realize that eschatology, the study of things to come, forms doctrines that make up a major segment of the Word of God. Bible eschatology (or prophecy) is critical to the Christian faith for three primary reasons:

- A full one-third of Scripture is prophetic.
- The Bible is the only sacred writing of the world's major religions that not only dares to predict the future, but does so with 100% accuracy.
- Therefore, it is by prophecy that God in His Word emphatically proves to man that He (God) alone is God.

Yet, Dr. Rick Warren not only discourages the study of Bible prophecy, but in his final segment of *40 Days of Peace* he declared that the study of prophecy is a waste of time. He claimed this to be the case because Matthew 24 teaches that when the *Gospel of the Kingdom* is preached in all the world, "the end shall come" and Jesus will set up His Kingdom. His point simply stressed to his followers that time spent studying prophecy is counter-productive when they could be out working on "Peace Programs" in their small groups. The problems with such philosophies are prolific (This subject was also briefly discussed in Chapter 2) :

- Will the P.E.A.C.E. Plan aid God in getting this *Gospel of the Kingdom* to the entire world?
- Are "we are in the business of building the Kingdom of God" as has been stated by Bob Buford, Leith Anderson, and others?
- What exactly is the *Gospel of the Kingdom*?
- What is "the end" of which Jesus was speaking?
- The Bible in the possession of this author states: *"All Scripture is given by inspiration of God and is profitable... that the man of God may be perfect, thoroughly furnished to all good works."* (31) and does not add the disclaimer, "that is, all Scripture except for that which pertains to prophecy." One would almost reason that Dr. Warren is concerned that his followers may learn some truth that contradicts his unscriptural position.

Dear friends, Christians in this Age of Grace cannot help build the Kingdom of God on Earth by preaching the Gospel of the Kingdom or doing any other great works. Does not Dr. Warren understand that "The Gospel of the Kingdom" is not equivalent to the "Gospel of Grace?" The true Gospel preached today is the "good news" of the death, burial, and resurrection of Jesus Christ by which He paid the price for mankind's crimes against God and redeemed Adam's lost race. Furthermore, all those who by grace through faith trust in His atoning blood through His death, burial, and resurrection for the forgiveness of sin will become the adopted sons of God to live with Him eternally in Heaven. This is the *Gospel of Grace.*

On the other hand, *The Gospel of the Kingdom* is the "good news" that the Kingdom of God is very near, and those who repent of their sins and turn to the King of Kings will become citizens of His earthly Kingdom. John the Baptist, Jesus, and His apostles preached this gospel to the House of Israel while He was on earth. However, the Jews rejected the Gospel of the Kingdom, and it will not again be correctly preached until God once again deals with Israel during the Tribulation period during the reign of Antichrist and the New World Order. Therefore, when Jesus spoke of the preaching of the Gospel of the Kingdom to the entire world before "the end," He was making reference to the 144,000 saved Jews who will preach this gospel in the Tribulation Period---not to anyone in this Age of Grace. (32)

In conclusion, that which is evidenced in the philosophies of the New Paradigm Church is the tragedy of faulty theology mixed with utopian systems concepts. In fairness, there are and have been many men of God who stand or stood in militant defense of the fundamentals of the Faith that embraced this same faulty eschatology, but these men never mixed this eschatology with occult utopian systems concepts. For when faulty eschatology marries utopian systems concepts, the new philosophies naturally and logically conceived of this union embrace the same "paradigm shift" of the occult world.

This trail can only lead to two possible conclusions to the matter. Dr. Warren and the others involved are either willing participants in a sinister conspiracy, or they have been duped into championing the cause of the utopian social planners to build their illustrious "heaven on earth." That is not to say that the intentions of most, including those of Dr. Warren himself, may not be honorable. Even Dr. Warren may rationalize the entire process by convincing himself of all those who could be saved in the process. However, in the final analysis, by following the current agenda of the Purpose-Driven, New Paradigm Church, there will be no construction of the Kingdom of God---only evangelical support and contribution to *Rebuilding the Tower of Babel.*

END NOTES

(1) Goldwater, Barry. *With No Apologies*, William Morrow Publishing, 1979, p.280.
(2) Revelation 13:12.
(3) Revelation 8-9.
(4) John 18:36.
(5) Dawkins, Peter. *Building Paradise*, Francis Bacon Research Trust, Warwickshire, UK, 2001, p.62
(6) Bailey, Alice. *Externalization of the Hierarchy*, Lucis Trust, New York, 1934.
(7) Wells, HG. *The New World Order*, As quoted by Marilyn Ferguson, *The Aquarian Conspiracy.*
(8) Dewey, John. Quotation from a speech to the American Education Fellowship, 1947.
(9) *Congressional Record.* April 24, 1954.

(10) Gardner, Richard. "The Hard Road to World Order", Foreign Affairs, April 1974.
(11) Commager, Henry Steele. "A Declaration of Interdependence", Signed by 32 U.S. Senators and 92 Representatives.
(12) Talbot, Strobe. "The Birth of the Global Nation", Time Magazine, July 20,1992.
(13) *Our Global Neighborhood, the Basic Vision.* United Nations Commission on Global Governance, p.46-47.
(14) Gorbachev, Mikhail."A Call for New Values", Noetic Sciences Review, Autumn, 1995.
(15) Earth Charter Benchmark Draft. www.earthcharter.org
(16) *Our Global Neighborhood, the Basic Vision.* p.9.
(17) "The New Group of World Servers". Pamphlet published by World Goodwill, Division of Lucis Trust, New York.
(18) Ibid.
(19) Matthew 23:27.
(20) Stafford, Tim. "The Business of the Kingdom," Christianity Today, 11/15/99.
(21) Ibid.
(22) Goldwater.
(23) Caldwell, Joseph G. *On Synarchy*, http://www.foundationwebsite.org/ July 27,2003.
(24) Gardner.
(25) This statement is based on an eyewitness account of an individual whose father, allegedly a member of an elite secret society, beginning in 1948 acted as the perpetrator and masqueraded as a Pentecostal minister in order to direct Pentecostals toward globalist goals
(26) Stafford.
(27) Ferguson, Marilyn. *The Aquarian Conspiracy*, J.P. Tarcher, Inc., Los Angeles, CA., 1980, p.377.
(28) Warren, Rick. *40 Days of PEACE*, Audio of sermon, Saddleback Community Church, 10/05.
(29) Dollar, George. *A History of Fundamentalism in America*, Bob Jones University Press, Greenville, SC. 1973. p.204.
(30) Goldstebin,Laurie. "Evangelicals Join Global Warming Initiative," *New York Times*, Feb. 8, 2006, www.nytimes.com.
(31) II Timothy 3:16.
(32) Matthew 24:14, Revelation 7:4-8.

Chapter 5

Am I My Brother's Leader?

Several years ago, this author was a member of an Independent Baptist Church whose direction shifted dramatically to the new paradigm thinking of Warren, Hybels, Southerland, and other prominent teachers of the seeker sensitive Church Growth Movement. After many struggles to maintain some level of purity within this assembly, a major battle developed when the pastor invited John Maxwell's Injoy Ministries to present its program for church numerical and financial growth. The bottom line of Injoy's proposal "guaranteed" that for the meager sum of $40,000 consulting service fee, the church would recoup a minimum of $300,000 over the two subsequent years from increased giving and church growth.

This was to be accomplished by systematically committing the entire existing congregation to a new "faith-promise" type of sacrificial "stewardship" program. This program would be presented to the church in predetermined segments:

- First, a slick marketing style video would get the entire congregation excited as to the possibilities for growth and complete financial stability.
- The details of the plan would then be presented to the church staff and higher profile, wealthier parishioners.
- Thirdly, the plan would be given to the "leadership of the church."
- After these groups of individuals were on board with the program, the rank and file membership would then receive the complete, detailed presentation. By the time the general membership was presented the plan for a vote, the die would be cast and the decision to go with Injoy sealed.

The third point is where this discussion gets interesting. For according to Dan Southerland in his book, *Transitioning, Leading Your Church Through Change,* "church leadership" should not only include the paid staff, deacons, Sunday School teachers, ushers, musicians, etc—but should also include those individuals with any level of influence that may adamantly oppose the plans for transition to the new paradigm model.

Therefore, the leaders of the church would not only include everyone who held an official office or distinct job in the church, but also those who were labeled as "trouble makers" who could undermine the entire effort.

What a concept! You appoint a potential "trouble maker" to a nebulous, innocuous, contrived leadership position, and effectively "buy" his or her allegiance by appealing to his or her ego.

Rick Warren reinforced this philosophy by stating in his *40 Days of Peace* series at Saddleback Community Church in the fall of 2005 that "everyone is a leader." As a matter of fact, Dr. Warren listed "*A Lack of Effective Leadership*" as one of mankind's major problems for which his P.E.A.C.E. Plan will provide a solution. A vital ingredient in his remedy to this so-called lack of leadership includes the "every individual is a leader" theory:

- Pastors lead their congregations
- Church officers lead the laity of the congregation
- Business professionals lead their companies
- Supervisors lead those in their groups of workers
- Every parent is a leader of his or her children
- Every individual has influence over at least one other individual, thus every individual is a "leader" in some respect.

Certainly there exists a certain degree of truth in this concept, and since (according to Dr. Warren) this problem of a "lack of effective leadership" ostensibly exists, does this mean that every individual needs to submit to "leadership training?" Furthermore, if one is dubbed a "leader," how could a "leader" possibly oppose the "vision" for the local church given to the pastor "by God Himself?" Additionally, of what will "leadership training" be comprised ---behavioral science, business management techniques, or even the principles of Eastern Religion? Is such training the mission of the Church? Does the Bible teach such a path for discipleship and edification? Is this a biblical approach, or is it in reality, simply an avenue for psychological manipulation? Will the army of "leaders" that emerges from P.E.A.C.E. programs direct a world-wide revival to "build the Kingdom of God," or to *Rebuild the Tower of Babel*?

THE LEADERSHIP OBSESSION

Over the last few years, the prominent players on the New Paradigm Church Game have become obsessed with this idea of developing "leaders" and teaching "leadership." These same individuals have become quite prolific in their writings on leadership and "volunteerism;" and the two seem to go hand-in-hand in the development of individuals to reach their maximum potential to assist in "building the Kingdom of God." The names that seem most prominent in this leadership movement include:

- Rick Warren, "America's Pastor" and pastor of Saddleback Community Church in Orange County, California.
- Ken Blanchard, noted author of *Lead Like Jesus* and other instructional books in corporate and church leadership. The services of Mr. Blanchard have also been retained to direct Saddleback's leadership programs.
- John Maxwell, a former pastor, author of many books on leadership, the founder of Injoy Ministries and the Maxwell Leadership Institute; is now considered one of the nation's foremost motivational and leadership experts.
- Bill Hybels, pastor of Willow Creek Community Church, Barrington, Illinois, has authored books on leadership and volunteerism.
- Andy Stanley, pastor of Northpointe Community Church, Atlanta, Georgia and the pastor of John Maxwell, is author of the book, *The Next Generation Leader.*
- Bob Buford, Texas communications giant and author of the book *Halftime,* is the director of the former Peter Drucker Foundation and the current Leadership Network.

While there are certainly others who deserve to be included on this list, these noted individuals will suffice as a sampling of the group of "evangelical Christians" absolutely obsessed with leadership. Further, when one reads the writings or listens to the sermons and lectures of these individuals regarding leadership, the lack of effective leadership, or leadership training; there is little or no variation in the content or the concepts. Logically, one must then conclude there must be a common denominator or several common denominators that unite this group of individuals to make their messages and methodologies echo as a choir singing in unison.

That said, if these very methodologies were based on the Word of God, this leadership obsession may well translate into a doctrinal position that every church should embrace. To that point, these individuals without exception, make the claim that their methodologies are in fact, based on the Word of God. However, any such claim is a masterfully choreographed exercise in deception and must be exposed as such before this obsession spreads any further through Evangelical and Fundamentalist Christianity. Before delving onto the source of the leadership obsession, perhaps a description of these methods need be explored in order to confirm to the reader of this manuscript their unbiblical nature.

THE SERVANT LEADER

Prior to diving into the details of leadership methodology, a disclaimer is necessary. Most of the principles of leadership discussed in this forum are not necessarily evil or even sinful. (Some aspects will be illustrated to have their origins in Luciferian philosophy, but this is certainly not the case in all instances.) Furthermore, to Dr. Warren's point, the world does indeed suffer from a lack of effective leadership in many arenas—including political, commercial, and religious--- but that does not give biblical *carte blanche* to the Church in adopting programs to train leaders that utilize unbiblical or extra-biblical principles to attain a predetermined outcome.

Additionally, commercial companies, corporations, and enterprises may be well served to adopt many of these very methods to enhance their business ethics, practices, and ultimately their incomes; but these same programs must be viewed from a strictly secular perspective that incorporates extreme caution to avoid syncretism of the sacred with the secular. Therefore, even in the case of these ostensibly beneficial principles, that which the Bible succinctly outlines in both the organizational structure and functional processes of the New Testament Church must be precisely followed. As a result, no matter how appropriate these extra-biblical, pseudo-biblical, or unbiblical leadership principles may or may not be in the corporate world, they have no place in the organization of the New Testament Church.

Distressingly, the afore-mentioned individuals who champion this cause are well-respected if not applauded in "conservative" evangelical circles.

Therefore, when these individuals claim the *Bible* as the source document for their leadership philosophies, most conservative evangelicals are not astute or discerning enough in their command of the Word of God to recognize Scripture taken out of context or completely misappropriated.

It is the misappropriation of the Word of God that raises extreme concern in this matter. A good definition of the misappropriation of the Word of God can most simply be termed as the misapplication of the Scripture into areas that a given passage does not pertain, or even the claim that the Bible supports a principle that it absolutely does not support. In other words, Hybels, Blanchard, Maxwell and the others make claims that the *Bible* teaches principles that it simply does not teach; or they claim that the *Bible* "says" something it simply does not "say." Such is the case in most aspects of the principle of *Servant Leadership*.

Servant Leadership is an outcome-based management technique based primarily on Peter Drucker's *Management by Objective.* The key points of *Servant Leadership* are as follows:

- The leader of an organization establishes the vision of the future. Peter Drucker stated that the vision of an organization should be no longer than can be written on the front of a t-shirt. This vision is not to be based on the enrichment of the leader at the expense of the followers, but the vision should be one that expresses rewards for the leader as well as the followers.
- The leader then "casts" the vision to his or her followers (employees, congregation, etc.) and motivates the followers to follow their leader to fulfill the vision.
- The leader does not rule over or oppress the followers, but the leader becomes a coach, a mentor, a facilitator, and a servant to insure that the followers make the vision of the leader their vision and claim ownership as their stake of the vision.
- The leader continues to teach the followers so that they know what the leader knows. By this process, the leader replicates himself or herself in the followers; and they become what is termed by Peter Drucker as *knowledge workers.* This principle is also well illustrated in the Amway pyramid marketing philosophy.
- By a constant casting of the vision, serving the followers to facilitate their obtaining the vision, and establishing ownership of the vision in

the hearts and minds of the followers; the servant leader maintains high morale, low turnover, and high productivity in the organization.
- As a result of all of the above, the vision is attained, a new vision is cast, and the process begins again.

This is the methodology of Servant Leadership, and this system unquestionably works. However, is this system biblical, or is it derived from other sources?

First, is the concept of "casting the vision" a Biblical principle, or an outcome-based tool for manipulation? The verse that so many who taunt leadership training based on "casting the vision" to support their philosophies is Proverbs 29:18:

"Where there is no vision, the people perish."

There are several interesting aspects of the embracing of this verse by the vision-minded Kingdom Builders:

- The verse is rendered this way only in the King James Version of the Old Testament. However, the New Paradigm philosophy regarding the KJV is one of complete distain. They view the KJV as archaic, outdated, and unappealing to today's postmodern mindset. Therefore, to adopt the very language of the KJV as opposed to the modern translations only confirms the hypocrisy of those who will grasp for any possible confirmation of their own predisposition.
- Actually, there is nothing wrong with the KJV translation of this verse. If the reader interprets the verse in its context, the contextual consideration of this passage makes it obvious that this passage is not describing a vision of a lofty goal or a designated outcome. Rather, the "vision" described in this verse is a prophetic vision---or the Word of God as received by the Old Testament prophets.
- A contextual rendering of the verse is better understood by restating it as *where there is no revelation of the Word of God (or prophetic vision), the people perish.*

The resulting truth is that the vision-casting servant leader is taking this verse completely out of its context, and is misappropriating the sacred

Scripture to force a description of a concept it does not, in reality, describe at all.

Bill Hybels, in his book, *Courageous Leadership*, is guilty of the same erroneous methodology on several occasions. One example of such misappropriation of the Word of God by Hybels is the twisting of Scripture in an attempt to "pigeonhole" the teachings of Jesus into an object lesson for an outcome-based church strategy:

> "Jesus...said, according to my translation of Matthew 28:29-30, 'Okay team, here's the goal: Go into all the world and preach the gospel. Lead every man, woman, and child to faith. Then grow them up by teaching them to observe all I have commanded you. Ready. Set. Go.' And they did.
>
> Part of the reason that Jesus' disciples turned the world upside down is that they had been commissioned by the world's greatest leader with the clearest, most exciting goal ever set: world redemption through the ministry of the church." (1)

In the first place, the Hybels translation of this verse is a complete misrepresentation of what the *Bible* relates of events subsequent to this command. Had Jesus actually said, "Ready...Set...Go...," the disciples completely forgot this commandment. For Acts Chapter 1 conveys that just prior to His ascension into Heaven, the disciples were anticipating the immediate establishment of the Millennial Kingdom. In addition to this major misconception, the disciples did not have the power, courage, or desire to "go into the world" until they were given the gift of the Holy Spirit as recorded in Acts 2.

Secondly, the commandment to "go and teach all nations" was just that---a commandment—not a goal; nor was this commandment part of the bigger goal of world redemption. The disciples were charged to obedience—not to reach a lofty goal. Jesus did not set goals or "cast a vision" for His followers. Rather, He demanded obedience to His commandments.

However, there were two specific factors that did indeed contribute to the proliferation of Christianity in the First Century:

- The disciples' commitment to obedience;
- More importantly, the power of the Holy Spirit working through the disciples and directly in the hearts of those who heard the Gospel.

Christianity did not sweep through the Roman Empire because human beings adopted a wildly successful outcome-based strategy of evangelism. Christianity swept the Empire only because the disciples were *obedient* to the Incarnate God and *empowered* by the very Holy Spirit of God Himself. This work of the Holy Spirit was simply a work in the hearts of those who were convicted by the preaching of the Word of God.

Pastor Hybels and the others obsessed with leadership strategies and training have forgotten the fact that the disciples, as well as modern Christians, are called to obedience to the Word of God. Such obedience then manifests itself in them as worthy vessels for the working of God's Holy Spirit through each one of them. *The Great Commission is not about human strategies and achievements---it is about the power of Almighty God revealed through His followers.* It is not about human achievements of those who deem themselves as leaders—it is about those who are willing to follow the commandments of the Lord Jesus Christ-- and through the "foolishness of preaching," enable the working of the Holy Spirit in the hearts of those who hear the precious truth of the Word of God.

Pastor Bill Hybels certainly does not possess a monopoly in the misappropriation of the Scripture. John Maxwell is another major player in this game. John Maxwell, who holds a Doctorate of Ministry from Fuller Theological Seminary, is the former pastor of Skyline Wesleyan Church in San Diego, California turned "leadership expert." He left the ministry to form The Injoy Group—a church consulting firm designed to help churches reach their full potential. Maxwell also heads the Maxwell Leadership Institute. This organization trains "leaders" worldwide with leadership seminars that employ headliners like occultist Mikhail Gorbechev and other such theologically questionable, well-known celebrities.

John Maxwell has written many books, but his *Maxwell Leadership Bible* exhibits multiple examples of the misappropriation of the Word of God.

The Maxwell Leadership Bible is a New King James Translation of the Scripture with commentary that relates to "leadership" in order to train "Christian leaders." The primary issue with this work is that the great majority of the commentary in the *Leadership Bible* is completely foreign to the context of the Word of God. While this venue will not be platform for a blow by blow account of the problems with Maxwell's commentary, a few random examples will be cited.

First, Dr. Maxwell misappropriates the Word of God in the book of Ezekiel in an attempt to promote "vision casting" and facilitation of the vision to the followers:

Vision: A Revelation Without Action Fades

> "God told Ezekiel to pack up his belongings and symbolically act out the exile awaiting the Jews using creative means to communicate vision.
>
> In Ezekiel 12:21-28, God speaks of the powerlessness of visions unless someone puts feet to them. Visions lose their strength without action to support them. Good leaders always share both the vision and the steps to their implementation.
>
> Yet the first step always must be to catch the God-given vision. Consider one process to go through as you attempt to catch God's vision for the people:
>
> - Look within you: What do you feel?
> - Look behind you: What have you learned?
> - Look around you: What is happening to others?
> - Look ahead of you: What is the big picture?
> - Look above you: What does God expect of you?
> - Look beside you: What resources are available to you?" (2)

The absurdity of this commentary not only denotes a misappropriation of the Word of God in an attempt to make applications outside of the context of the Scripture but also inserts principles of humanistic psychology and behavioral science masquerading as biblical principles. Actually, Dr. Maxwell needs to have several questions asked of him in respect to this commentary:

- Exactly where does Ezekiel relate that this passage is a lesson in creative vision-casting?
- At what point does one seek God's vision in the pages of His revealed Word, and why would that not be the first thing an individual seeking God's vision would do?
- If seeking God's vision, why would one look inside himself or seek human knowledge at all? Isn't this the methodology of the occult and Eastern Religion?
- When does one fall on his face before God and humbly seek God's will? Is this the same as a "look above?"

The answers to these questions reveal a major problem with the entire "leadership training" process: *Not only is this process NOT based on the Word of God, but it is based on human behavioral science.* If then it is not based on the Word of God, what place does it have in the Church? Better yet, what place does it have as commentary in the *Bible*?

An example from the New Testament in Maxwell's Bible reveals another such commentary:

Team Building: Jesus Assembled a Team to Own a Vision

> "One could argue that Jesus constructed the most important team ever assembled...He saw Matthew's potential to become an apostle and a writer: Jesus never felt bound by human opinion or approval...He treated individuals based on their future potential, not present status.
>
> In the same way, we must free ourselves from the boundaries that keep us from building a balanced team. Consider some questions we might learn from Jesus:
>
> - What positive qualities exist that might be seen as negative behavior?

- Do the individuals show initiative even if it has been misdirected?
- Would these people add positive chemistry and unique value if placed on the team?
- Are they hungry to become something more than they are now?
- Do they demonstrate compassion that could be redirected?
- Could they play a needed role on the team?" (3)

In the first place, *Jesus did not and does not deal in "potential."* Jesus did not see potential in His disciples, for Jesus knew the future--- He was fully aware of his disciples' future just as He is with Christians today---He saw not only the present but also the future. He knew what each of them would do and become in the future; for Jesus of Nazareth was (and is) the Incarnate God. Therefore, to use Jesus as the pattern for leadership by asking Dr. Maxwell's six questions listed in this commentary is completely irrelevant when following the example set by Jesus. These questions have their origin in human behavioral science---not the example of the Incarnate God.

The final illustration from the *Maxwell Leadership Bible* is a recurrent theme throughout the writings of the entire group of "Kingdom Builders" of the New Paradigm Church--- the humanization of Jesus Christ:

> *"Jesus often left the demands of his work to come apart and pray. He used this solitude to regain perspective and once more see the big picture… "* (4)

Please excuse the informality of this next statement, but *you have got to be kidding me*! Why do men like John Maxwell, Rick Warren, Bob Buford, Bill Hybels, Andy Stanley, and the others playing the New Paradigm Church Game all apparently feel a compulsion to bring Jesus Christ down to the level of mere mortals? Why do they not understand that Jesus did not need to find a "safe place" to "regain perspective" or "see the big picture?" Does Fuller Seminary not teach that Jesus Christ is God? Do they think their constituents need a humanized savior who must resort to the techniques of behavioral science or risk failure of his mission?

Additionally, why do these individuals ascribe the leadership principles of human behavioral science disguised as the dictates of the Word of God?

In response to these questions, the following observations must be made:

- The *Bible* does not teach that Christian leaders are to cast a "vision" to their followers and facilitate an outcome-based process to attain the vision.
- The *Bible* actually has very little to say about leadership. It does have a lot to say about following---following the commandments of Jesus, the commandments of the Scriptures, and the direction of the Holy Spirit.
- Jesus did not engage in team-building exercises, cast a vision for world evangelism, and absolutely did not make self assessments to insure reaching His full potential.

So what assessment should be made of the matter? Christians need discernment. Christians need to assess everything by the standard of the Word of God. Christians then need to question any individual who departs from or misappropriates biblical principles. An example of just this type of questioning was presented by Bill Hybels in his book, *Courageous Leadership*. Pastor Hybels recorded (to the surprise of this author) a question posed to him in a "leadership seminar:"

> "Bill, I do not think you should mix best management practices with spiritual stuff…I'm really uneasy with all of this leadership training, leadership development, and managing for results I see at Willow. I think that when it comes to God, the spiritual realm, and the church, it ought to be laissez-faire. Hands off. Let go and let God. That's what I think." (5)

This individual's "laissez-faire" terminology is not as this author would term the organization of the local church, nor could complete agreement be made with his "hands off, let go, and let God" when the Word of God dictates the principles and methods that govern the local church. However, the questioner is completely justified in his uneasiness with the assessment of business management and leadership training at Willow Creek. Pastor Hybel's response should have made this individual even more uneasy:

> "What you have to understand is that some of us church leaders believe to the core of our beings that the local church is the hope of the world...We believe that the church addresses every human beings deepest need. We believe that the church can lead people into a whole new way of living and loving and serving, and can thereby transform society...we are so determined to get our visions right...and come up with successful strategies...*That's why we make no apology for learning and applying the best practice principles as God leads us in our churches...*"(6)

Is Pastor Hybels saying that God leads him to the utilization of psychology, human potential, human behavioral sciences, and blatant manipulation in directing his ministry? Are these strategies superior to God's plan for the Church as given in the New Testament? Obviously, this is precisely what he is saying; but where will such a strategy lead?

To determine the direction leadership strategies are actually taking, more questions must be considered from a biblical context:

- Should the same principles that apply to secular leadership apply to Christian leaders?
- Should not any vision given by God come directly from the pages of the Word of God?
- Will God ever convey a vision that contradicts the commands of His Word?
- Is a humanistic plan or God's direction the best for the Church?
- In order to make a humanistic plan best for the Church, would not Jesus need to be humanized?
- Did Jesus actually call every Christian to be a *Servant Leader*—or a servant follower?

LEAD LIKE JESUS

When Dr. Rick Warren announced in 2005 that Ken Blanchard would join the Saddleback Team to implement the leadership portion of the P.E.A.C.E. Plan, he was met with a firestorm of criticism. Those who raised the loudest protests contended that Blanchard was a "New Age Guru." The evidence against Blanchard was very convincing and well documented:

- He wrote the foreword to Jim Ballard's *Mind Like Water*
- He wrote the foreword to Franz Metcalf's *What Would Buddha Do At Work?*
- His endorsement is on the front cover of *The Corporate Mystic*
- His endorsement is on the back cover of Deepak Chopra's *7 Spiritual Laws of Success*
- He wrote the Foreword to Ellen Tadd's (clairvoyant) book, *Death and Letting Go*. (7)

This is indeed a very incriminating list, and does indicate that Mr. Blanchard has at a minimum endorsed New Age and occult teachings.

However, Dr. Warren came to his defense by claiming that Ken Blanchard's life had been changed by his faith in Jesus Christ, and he did many things prior to his "crossing the line of faith" that he not only regretted, but also repented of these things. Therefore, in spite of a nagging distrust of anything Dr. Warren may contend, this author will not attempt to discredit Mr. Blanchard based on his past endorsements or associations. Rather, this manuscript will only briefly deal with a few of the philosophies and statements of Ken Blanchard's "Christian leadership" book that is the foundation of the servant leadership philosophy, *Lead Like Jesus*. (Even though this section will be brief, just the few segments discussed here will leave no doubt as to the serious issues communicated by the *Lead Like Jesus* program. In addition to his book, Ken Blanchard has trained thousands of individuals worldwide with his *Lead Like Jesus* seminars.)

To restate the previous disclaimer when addressing Mr. Blanchard's work, much of his material may be very useful in the secular world; and its concepts may also represent a commendable moral improvement in many of the high rise (or low rise) corporate structures. However, the main concerns are very similar to those already discussed:

- The misappropriation of the Word of God
- The humanization of Jesus Christ by concepts that assault His deity

- The misapplication of humanistic, secular, or occult principles to the Church

When Blanchard begins his book, *Lead Like Jesus*, he makes some personal comments in the introduction:

- He identifies himself as a behavioral scientist.
- He claims that Jesus performed to perfection all the principles of effective leadership that he (Blanchard) had taught for the past 35 years.
- He was also fascinated with how Jesus transformed 12 ordinary and unlikely people into the "first generation leaders of a movement that continues to affect the course of world history." (8)

A very cursory analysis of this small portion to the introduction of the book reveals the major dark undercurrents that run throughout this entire philosophy:

- Ken Blanchard reveals the perspective of his thesis—He is a behavioral scientist. That means he deals in human potential, positive thinking, psychological manipulation, and the general human behaviors as viewed within a psychological framework. Thus his perspective is not biblical, but humanistic.
- If Jesus "performed to perfection" the principles he (Blanchard) taught for 35 years, does this mean Jesus also approached His leadership of the apostles and other disciples from a humanistic perspective? Also as an aside, does this statement not negate the claim made by Dr. Warren that Blanchard is a changed man? For if Jesus performed to perfection all that Blanchard taught for 35 years, would this include (to pick a name totally at random) the *7 Spiritual Laws for Success* by occultist Deepak Chopra and endorsed by Mr. Blanchard?
- Finally, had Jesus resorted to behavioral science to transform these 12 unlikely people to leadership mega-stardom, exactly where does that leave His deity? Did Jesus not possess the eternal omnipotence of Almighty God? If that were the case, why would he resort to humanistic manipulation? Again, as with the other leadership-obsessed "Kingdom Builders," Ken Blanchard pulls the Incarnate God down to the human level in order to better relate to the current postmodern culture.

- To reinforce this perspective, later in his book Blanchard claims that Jesus had the 3 inner-circle apostles—Peter, James, and John—"to lean on in crucial times." (9) Let's please clarifiy this once and for all: *Jesus did not need to lean on anyone. Again, no matter what these men may or may not think, Jesus was (and is) the Incarnate God,* and the assembly of the "inner circle" of apostles was for their benefit---not Jesus' emotional stability.

Blanchard echoes Hybels and Maxwell in discussing the transformation of the disciples after 3 years of Jesus' leadership. Another example of the misappropriation of Scripture is evidenced when Philip was told by Jesus just prior to the Crucifixion, *"Have I been so long time with you, and yet you have not known me, Philip?"* (10) Blanchard, like the others, is teaching a new generation of evangelicals that the strategies and procedures taught by business management professions are superior to the working of the Holy Spirit in lives. It is true that Philip became a great evangelist, but as illustrated here, his experience with Jesus without the direction and indwelling of the Holy Spirit had not equipped him to perform the tasks ahead.

As a final example, Mr. Blanchard resorts to wild speculation in an attempt to make Jesus fit into the behavioral science mold. He claims that the experiences of Jesus in the carpenter shop "provided him with a practical model for growing and developing people that He was able to use to guide the learning experience of His disciples from calling to commission."(11) Blanchard details this model as a 4-tier learning stage: 1) Novice, 2) Apprentice, 3) Journeyman, and 4) Master.

Dear friends, this is pure speculative nonsense. In the first place, there is no Scriptural evidence Jesus ever worked in Joseph's carpenter shop. Secondly, where does this 4-step process originate? Even if Jesus did work in the carpenter shop, where is the documentation that He traversed this systemic path? Lastly, and most importantly, *Jesus did not need a practical model for teaching His disciples.* Jesus, as God, had all of the knowledge, wisdom, and power of the universe at His disposal---the very thought that He needed a model developed by some mere mortal as a learning aid is not only preposterous, but is also another affront to His deity.

Therefore, if this leadership scenario is the philosophy that Ken Blanchard brings to Dr. Rick Warren's P.E.A.C.E. Plan to train millions of Christians in the United States, Rwanda, and worldwide--- true Christianity that holds to the Fundamental Doctrines of the Faith better be well prepared for the most deceptive war that those who seek to defend the Faith have ever faced. For the P.E.A.C.E. Plan will seek to meet the physical needs of millions of individuals without doctrine. It will implement the Theosophical plan of Alice Bailey—"knowing without doctrine." It may well become the plan used to fulfill the vision of Lucis Trust and World Goodwill---to work goodwill to all men and bring about the occult (not biblical) Kingdom of God on Earth. Intentionally or unintentionally, the armies of *Servant Leaders* will be marching across the globe to fulfill a globalist agenda.

TRANSFORMATIONAL LEADERSHIP AND GENERAL SYSTEMS THEORY

The questions revolving around the principles of the *Servant Leader* must be explored on a deeper level if one were to adopt the philosophy that everyone is a leader as Dr. Warren contends. This exploration goes away and beyond the earlier discussion that involves just the local church. It must also be viewed from a global perspective based not only on the far-reaching influence of men like Dr. Rick Warren, John Maxwell, Bill Hybels, and the ghost of Peter Drucker; but also other "darker entities" who are promoting the same agenda. Most significantly, these "darker entities" are not only promoting the same agenda, but actually are the originators of these very concepts.

A study of the agendas and goals of organizational entities that include the Fabian Socialists of the early 20th Century, the United Nations, and occult organizations such as Lucis Trust are very revealing when one begins to consider and analyze the effects on society if a significant number of individuals begin to consider themselves as "servant leaders." Additionally, if these "servant leaders" seek to indoctrinate those over which they may exert influence in the outcome-based principles of General Systems Theory (GST), the global impact could be potentially staggering.

As described by the authors of the occult treatise, *Spiritual Politics*, "systems thinking" of General Systems Theory is a key tenet of the so-called *Ageless Wisdom* promoted by H.P. Blavatsky, Alice Bailey, and the Lucis Trust. *Spiritual Politics* details the origins of GST by stating:

> "...popularized by biologist Ludwig von Bertalanffy, who was in turn inspired by the 15th Century cardinal and mystic Nicholas of Cusa...It means seeing relationships rather than only linear cause and effect chains and seeing processes of change rather than snapshots of change as management consultant and author Peter Senge notes..." (12)

No wonder US business leaders in the 1940s labeled Peter Drucker's systems approach in his *Management by Objective* philosophies as "German mysticism." As repeatedly noted in this manuscript, Drucker was no stranger to the likes of Kingdom Builders Warren, Hybels, and Buford; and neither is Peter M. Senge, who is mentioned above. Senge's book, *The Fifth Discipline* is sold on Rick Warren's *pastors.com.*, and at least one article by Senge is also posted at the time of this writing on this same website.

Even more interestingly, the authors of *Spiritual Politics* have a lot to say about what they term "transformational leadership." They state that this transformational leadership is the basis for the leadership of what they term the *New World Order.* Note the relationship of this principle to that of those evangelicals who are obsessed with leadership and leadership training:

> "Where there is a good synthesis of hierarchy and democracy (a social democracy –ed.), leaders accept only as much authority as people are willing to give them. *Work gets done through inspiring people with vision or purpose.* (emphasis added) (13)

Let's see..."vision" and "purpose"...Where have we heard those terms before? Surely this must be purely coincidental. Right? Surely conservative Evangelicals would never adopt the methodologies and terminologies of those who are adepts in the occult sciences and "black arts." ...or would they? Who are these people underneath the whitewashed outer façade of conservative evangelicalism? Is this really yet another coincidence?

Spiritual Politics, written in 1994 is endorsed inside the cover by well-known occultists David Spangler and Willis Harman with the forward written by the Dalai Lama. This book is heralded on its cover as "cutting edge stuff that takes up where *The Aquarian Conspiracy* left off." The concepts are consistently promoting "a new paradigm," a "new world order," and communitarian principles. Additionally, and most importantly for the purposes of this discussion, this book describes its so called "transformational leadership" in the same terms as do Drucker, Senge, Hybels, Stanley, Buford, Maxwell, and Warren! Is this more mere coincidence? With the possible coincidences previously discussed in this manuscript, how many coincidences can one tolerate before this series of events evolves into something closer to conspiracy than coincidence? When one then introduces organizations like the Lucis Trust, the Fabian Socialists, or even the United Nations into the discussion---Where will this trail of "coincidences" lead?

When one follows the trail of coincidences, it leads right back to these very organizations, and the agendas of these organizations all include significant similarities:

- They all hold to worldview that embraces a world system of Global Governance and a reduction or elimination of national sovereignty.
- There is a common recognition that government and business will not be equipped to support the demands of any socialist democracy, so the burden must be borne by the social or nonprofit sector.
- If the social or non-profit sector of society must bear this burden, the main support of the burden must be borne not by a paid labor force, but rather, by an army of *volunteers.*

Consider further these points in light of the new emerging "global economy" based on the social democracy and today's realities:

- More socialistic demands for increased government intervention into the private sector continue to escalate.
- Demands for instant shareholder profits in the corporate world apply more pressure for new and extended low cost labor sources.
- As domestic manufacturing migrates to the low cost labor pools of Asia, Eastern Europe, and Africa to support the pressure for

exponential increase in corporate profits to shareholders, the reduced tax base to support the services provided by a more socialistic government could lead to total economic collapse.

- Thus, the insertion of displaced workers into corporate and government programs as *volunteers* living off a "bare subsistence" income effectively supports the new order or "community" created by systems-oriented social planners. (i.e.-- virtual slave labor)

THE AGE OF THE VOLUNTEER

Before one begins to conclude that this author has completely his mind, consider what Annie Bessant, the Director of the occultist Theosophical Society between the tenure of Blavatsky and Bailey stated:

> "This, however, hardly solves the general question as to the apportioning of laborers to the various forms of labor, but a solution has been found...Leaving young men and women free to choose their employments, he would equalize the rates of *volunteering* by equalizing the attractions of the trades." (14)

In other words, if working for a living is made less attractive by social programs or less available by moving industry to lower cost labor pools, the attractiveness of becoming a volunteer (or slave) is greatly enhanced. To be more blunt, the fact is that this scenario has already been planned by occult globalists, and "trial balloons" of this philosophy have been floated since the 1960s. A minute sampling of these "trial balloons" include:

- The Peace Corps
- United Nations Public-Private Partnerships
- The Points of Light Foundation
- Americorps
- USA Freedom Corps

These are but a very few of the initiatives and programs to promote volunteerism. If one were to browse on any search engine on the internet for the word "volunteerism," thousands of items become available to the browser. Some of these programs are very well known, and as stated earlier, there are certainly praiseworthy aspects of many of these programs.

However, there are some aspects of government-sponsored volunteerism that cannot help but cause at least one "raised eyebrow:"

- The name of the Points of Light Foundation as developed by President George Bush I is derived from a quotation by Fabian occultist H.G. Wells who stated, "...a planned world-state is appearing *at a thousand points...* " (15)
- Occultist Alice Bailey reveals that the "Points of Light" refers to the members of a subgroup of Lucis Trust—The New Group of World Servers, and claims that 1934 marked the beginning of "the organizing of the men and women... group work of a new order... [with] *progress defined by service... the world of the Brotherhood... the Forces of Light...* [and] out of the spoliation of all existing culture and civilization, the new world order must be built." (16)
- The leader of the Communitarian Movement, Amitai Etzioni, was instrumental in organizing Americorps. Communitarians believe that mandatory volunteerism in the community is a moral obligation of all citizens ---This belief was shared by H.G. Wells, Annie Bessant, Alice Bailey, and now is championed by President Bush II. (17)
- The USA Freedom Corps of President Bush II unites Americorps and the Peace Corp with the Senior Corps into one behemoth bureaucratic organization. President Bush is asking that *every American* donate 2 years of their remaining lifetime to governmental volunteer services. (18)

Other names that crop up in this discussion include Nelson Rockefeller. He stated:

> "...with voluntary service...and our dedicated faith in the brotherhood of all mankind...sooner perhaps than we can realize...there will evolve the basis for a federal structure of the free world." (19)

Mr. Rockefeller's statement goes a long way toward a complete summation of the thought process behind government–sponsored (or mandated) volunteerism. If there were such a thing as the "universal brotherhood of man," or a true "community of humanity," these concepts would possess some credibility. However, the truth of the matter is that these concepts are a direct lie of Lucifer. For humanity is made up of two distinct segments of individuals---the children of God and the children of Lucifer. These two groups do share the planet, have the same physical needs, and must work in tandem in mundane matters. However, there is a great spiritual gulf that divides the two, and Christians must understand that the brotherhood of man under the fatherhood of God concept is false.

Does this mean that Christians are to turn a blind eye or a deaf ear to the problems mankind faces as a whole? Certainly not, and Christians are commanded to reach out with the Word of God in concern for the spiritual condition of every individual. However, to participate in globalistic programs and support the causes that are attempting to fulfill the goals for a New World Order is contrary to the directives of Scripture for those that are born again.

TRUE MINISTRY OR VOLUNTEERISM?

It is for this very reason that one must question the Kingdom Builders of the New Paradigm Church when they align themselves with global systems engineers and planners. Pastor Bill Hybels has written a book on the magnificent virtues and benefits of volunteerism, but a serious question needs to be presented to Pastor Hybels and the other leadership-obsessed elite of this group.

Are those who participate in unpaid positions of ministry truly volunteers?

If one were to define a volunteer in this day as one who receives a modest remuneration or no tangible payment for services rendered, then the answer to this question is an emphatic *NO!* The *Bible* is clear that God is a God of justice. God does not enslave His servants here on the earth, but He loves them and blesses them even in this lifetime. Additionally, the *Bible* succinctly teaches that any work done in the name of Jesus will surely be rewarded--- not only on Earth, but also abundantly in Heaven.

Therefore, God's servants in ministry *are not volunteers*. The *Bible* states, "Eye hath not seen, nor ear heard, nor hath it entered into to the heart of man; the things that God has prepared for them that love Him." No unpaid volunteers are described in this statement. The ministry of God is the highest-paying job on Earth. It may be true, that temporary, sacrificial investments may be made by this group, and certainly these individuals called of God to the ministry are not "in it for the money." However, the rewards will be dispersed, and the just God will convey upon His children the windfall profits of righteous living that will eternally prove that they are royal joint-heirs with Jesus Christ--not unpaid volunteers.

NEW PARADIGM LEADERS AND VOLUNTEERS

So where is this all leading, and how does it all correlate? Here is the heart of the matter:

- If everyone is a leader, and everyone must fulfill a moral obligation of volunteerism, the Kingdom Builders of the New Paradigm Church are assembling an army of volunteers who have been given the manipulative leadership training of the humanistic behavioral scientist.
- As a result of this training, the volunteer army has a low view of Jesus Christ, a great deal of self-esteem, and no concept of sin or true repentance---much less any other Fundamental doctrine of the Scriptures.
- Additionally, this army is willing to blindly follow the vision casters in the group that claim to be pursuing God's vision. However, in the absence of doctrinal preaching and teaching, this army has now been primed to fall for any false teaching that is touted as "God's vision."
- This gullibility for false teaching is already evidenced by the globalistic "systems thinking" becoming tantamount in the New Paradigm Church. The army of leader/volunteers is at this moment under the influence of teachers who, at best, are educating them in occult terminologies and concepts in the name of Evangelical Christianity. At worst...that will be discussed in the next and final chapter of this book.

In conclusion, and as has been stated in this manuscript, *true, Bible-based Christianity is on the very precipice of becoming virtually nonexistent.* Those displaced believers who separated from the new paradigm churches and are seeking a solid Bible-believing church are becoming more frustrated with each passing day. Churches that formerly stood for the truth of the Word of God are now jumping on the bandwagon by the thousands to cash in on the purpose-driven, vision-casting, new paradigm windfall.

More distressingly, what of those who are blindly following the vision-casting Pied Pipers of the New Paradigm? Are these individuals truly born again, or has a watered-down gospel and absence of doctrinal preaching led them to a sense of false security? Will these individuals be the very ones that make up those who will be deceived at the rise of Antichrist as he proclaims Messianic rule over the "Kingdom of God?" In spite of their best intentions, are the Kingdom Builders of the New Paradigm Church who think they are training servant leaders to usher in the Kingdom of God actually recruiting and assembling an army of volunteers to *Rebuild the Tower of Babel?*

ENDNOTES

(1) Hybels, Bill. *Courageous Leadership*, Zondervan, Grand Rapids, MI, 2002, p.90.
(2) Maxwell, John. *The Maxwell Leadership Bible*, Thomas Nelson, Nashville, TN, 2002, p.977.
(3) Ibid. p.1201.
(4) Ibid. p.1200.
(5) Hybels. p.69.
(6) Ibid. p.70.
(7) http://www.lighthousetrailsresearch.com/PressReleasekenblanchard.htm
(8) Blanchard, Ken. *Lead Like Jesus*, Thomas Nelson Publishers, Nashville, TN, 2005, pp. XII-XIII.
(9) Ibid. p.183.
(10) John 14:8-9.
(11) Blanchard. p.129.
(12) McLaughlin, Corinne. *Spiritual Politics*, Balentine Books, New York, 1994, p.88.
(13) Ibid.p.99.
(14) Bessant, Annie. *The Organization of Society, Industry under Socialism*, paragraph II.2.16.
(15) Wells, HG. *Experiment in Autobiography*, 1935.
(16) Bailey, Alice. *The Externalization of the Hierarchy*, Lucis Publishing, New York, 1934.
(17) Raapana, Niki. "What is a Communitarian?" www.jewishtribalreview.org/raapana.htm.
(18) Bush, George W. "State of the Union Address," 2002.
(19) Rockefeller, Nelson. *The Future of Federalism: The Godkin Lectures at Harvard University* 1962, Harvard University Press, 1962, p.82.

Chapter 6

Building the One-World Church

The Great Man rose to his feet. An overwhelming silence permeated the immense crowd as an ocean wave over the sand of the seashore. The silence rose in a hushed crescendo of anticipation as he motioned to the high priest. The priest slowly lifted his staff, and a mountain of fire fell from the sky, exploding into a raging inferno. The huge crowd stood mesmerized as the prepared sacrifice was incinerated in the flames. The silence then erupted into choruses of praise as every individual fell prostrate to the earth in humble, yet fearful worship of the Great Man.

Is this not the long-anticipated Holy One? Is this not the Second Coming of Christ to the Christian, Krishna to the Hindu, Quetzelcoatl to the New Ager, Maitreya to the Buddhist, the Imam Mahdi to the Muslim, Hiram Abiff to the Mason, and Messiah ben David to the Jew? Is he not the fulfillment of the ancient prophecies concerning each of these and others? After all, he alone accomplished what all before failed to achieve: *He became the provider of world peace, produced incontrovertible evidence establishing himself as the rightful priest-king of all mankind, and enabled both spiritual and political direction for the entire planet.* With all the dissenters humanely removed from the planet to rethink their positions, he successfully blended the common values of all religions into a new, syncretistic, all-encompassing faith. The long-awaited "Golden Age" had at last arrived... *Welcome to the One-World Church.*.

This Super Church will not appear out of thin air, as the plans for this organization are as old as the present post-diluvian civilization itself. It further will not result from a direct frontal assault on established religion; but rather, it will be built piece by piece-- moving in a series of "baby steps" as the mending of subplots in a complex mystery novel. The pieces are now falling into place, and the subplots are rushing headlong to the climax—the Rapture of the Church and subsequent appearance of Antichrist. Tragically, many well-meaning, sincere individuals are falling prey to the vast deception of Lucifer's plan for the Super Church. This includes many Christians and Christian organizations who are becoming unwitting accomplices to the impending One World Church and its political half-sister, the New World Order.

How could any Christian be so naive? How could God possibly allow His children to contribute to the plans of Lucifer? Based on what has been written to this point in this manuscript, evidence has been presented that indicates an individual will not resist that which he perceives as good, just, or even holy. At the heart of the issue lies the fact that when a man is born-again, he does not mystically become immune to deception. Even more tragically, when individuals are given a false gospel--or are enrolled into a religious program that manipulates them to a false perception of salvation; these individuals may as well attach a large, bright red target painted over their hearts--for they are set up and primed to become members in an army of volunteer drones marching to the drumbeat of the ultimate and consummate false leader.

The question posed by this manuscript is very simple: Are the leaders of the seeker-sensitive, purpose-driven, "New Paradigm Church" actually preparing unsuspecting throngs of sincere individuals into either supporting or actually participating in what will become the Super Church of Antichrist?

Over the course of this manuscript, many "coincidences" have been noted to produce "circumstantial evidence" that the program of the Church of the New Paradigm is doing exactly that. In order to better organize the thoughts of the reader, a concise list of these "coincidences" can be restated as follows:

- Rick Warren illustrated the events at the Tower of Babel as something positive.
- The "group-think" philosophies of the "meta-church" are a carbon copy of those touted by occult organizations like the Lucis Trust.
- Shades of pantheism appear in Rick Warren's best-selling "devotional book," *The Purpose-Driven Life.*
- The 3 core principles of witchcraft and goddess worship: *immanence, interconnection, and community--* as listed by Starhawk are predominantly taught by Rick Warren in *The Purpose-Driven Life;* and one or more of these principles are predominate themes in his *40 Days of Community* and *40 Days of PEACE.*

- Rick Warren's *World Class Christian* in *The Purpose-Driven Life* is described with the same phrases and in the same context as those who condone neo-pagan environmental globalism and describe themselves as "world beings."
- Fuller Seminary's Dr. Donald McGavaran's *Homogenous Unit Principle* aligns perfectly with the Gnostic conversion methodology of the Knights Templar, while coming into direct opposition with the methodology of the Word of God.
- Dr. Rick Warren utilizes the globalistic terminology, *Declaration of Interdependence* in his *40 Days of Community* program.
- Many similarities of Marilyn Ferguson's *Aquarian Conspiracy* and Corinne McLaughlin's *Spiritual Politics* appear in Rick Warren's *The Purpose-Driven Life.*
- The group-think concepts of Carl George in *The Coming Church Revolution* are distressingly similar to those of Marilyn Ferguson, H.G. Wells, Alice Bailey, and other occultists.
- Rick Warren's emphasis on building relationships and the need for "community" echoes the writings of Alice Bailey who wrote via automatic writing under the influence of a demonic "spirit guide."
- The Kingdom of God rhetoric of the New Paradigm Church leaders mirrors the occult philosophy of the Kingdom of God taught by H.P. Blavatsky, H.G. Wells, Alice Bailey, and the Lucis Trust.
- The "building community" model of New Paradigm utopian social planner Peter Drucker equates not only to the plan of the globalist Trilateral Commission, but also to that of 19th Century occultist, Alexandre Saint Yves d'Alveydre.
- Rick Warren, Leith Anderson, and others have united philosophically with pagan environmentalists by signing the Evangelical Climate Initiative.
- The vast majority of "biblical" references for servant leadership are not biblical at all, but hinge on the principles of behavioral science.
- Jesus in a leadership role is offensive to no one. It is Jesus the Redeemer that is the stumbling block to the entire world.
- Pastor Bill Hybels implies that God leads him to the use of psychology, human potential, human behavioral sciences, and blatant manipulation in directing his ministry.
- John Maxwell incorporates humanistic and Eastern religious methodology into the commentary presented in his *Leadership Bible.*

- All of the leaders of the New Paradigm Church have a distinct tendency to humanize and thereby attack the deity of Jesus Christ.
- The "vision" and "purpose" terminology of the "Ageless Wisdom" aligns with the methodologies and terminologies of Warren, Blanchard, Maxwell and the other leaders of the New Paradigm movement.
- Peter Drucker's 1942 book, *The Future of the Industrial Man* was termed "German mysticism" by Henry Hazlitt writing in the Winter 1943 edition of the *Yale Review*.
- Rick Warren endorses and promotes Peter Senge on his pastors.com website.

Even the most skeptical reader must admit that this is a long list of "coincidences;" and as noted earlier, when coincidence after coincidence occurs within any movement or philosophy, that movement or philosophy must be called into question as to its integrity. Furthermore, the integrity of the leaders of such a movement or philosophy must also be closely scrutinized. The fact of the matter is that the integrity of neither the New Paradigm Church movement nor its leaders fare too well when the facts are objectively examined, and there is even more evidence to examine.

LADIES HOME JOURNAL

Among the additional evidence is even another "coincidence" that occurred in March of 2005 when *Ladies Home Journal* published Rick Warren's article, *Learn to Love Yourself.* (1) In this article, Dr. Warren proposed "5 truths" that "form the basis of a healthy self image." These five truths are as follows:

- *Accept Yourself* – Dr. Warren states that God accepts all women unconditionally, so they in turn should accept themselves.
- *Love yourself* – Dr. Warren here states that women should love themselves because God unconditionally loves them.
- *Be true to yourself* – By being true to yourself, Dr. Warren stresses that one should build on her strengths while managing her weaknesses.
- *Forgive yourself* – Dr. Warren apparently believes that asking forgiveness of God equates to self forgiveness.

- *Believe in yourself* --- Women should practice self affirmation in order to convince themselves of their self worth, capabilities, and value.

These truths in reality, are not truths at all; but rather, these principles are based in humanistic psychology, and humanistic psychology is planted in diametric opposition to the Word of God.

In response to this article, here are some questions for Dr. Warren:

- Does God accept us unconditionally? Does not the Bible teach that mankind is only acceptable to God by the merits of Jesus Christ and His shed blood?
- Is God's unconditional love an indicator of our own self worth or the revelation that God's love is independent of our depraved nature?
- Does the Word of God teach that one is to build on his or her strengths and manage their weaknesses, or is God's strength is made perfect in our weaknesses? Did not the Apostle Paul state, "My strength is made perfect in weakness... for when I am weak, then I am strong?" (2)
- If an individual needs to be so devoted to self, so absorbed with self, and so focused on self---how can that individual follow the commandments of Jesus Christ and the teachings of the Word of God?
- Did not Jesus say that the individual who follows Him is subject to self-denial?
- If self esteem is so critical, why does the Bible teach that we are to "esteem others higher than ourselves?"
- Most suspiciously, if a conservative Southern Baptist preacher is given the opportunity to write a column in a national publication, why would that preacher use this platform to promote principles of humanistic psychology that contradict the principles of the Word of God, and never once mention the name of Jesus ?

After careful consideration of the obvious answers to these questions, one must add the prolific exposition of the Self Esteem Gospel made so popular by Norman Vincent Peele and Robert Schuler in the *Ladies Home Journal* to the long list of coincidences that would lead one to question any biblical connection between the Church of the New Paradigm and the local Church as described in the New Testament.

THE ATTACK ON FUNDAMENTALISM

As noted earlier in this book, Christian Fundamentalists have come under heavy attack in the past few years simply due to the prolific use of the term "fundamentalist" by the secular news media. Christian Fundamentalists have become equated with the radical, militant Islamic Fundamentalists and cast in the public media as something between dangerous, psychotic lunatics and fascist, extremist terrorists who want to seize control of the government of the United States.

The reality of the situation is that neither extreme (nor anything between these extremes) could be further from reality, and the only similarity between the Christian Fundamentalist and the Islamic Fundamentalist is the existence of a common, unshakable allegiance to their respective scriptures and a desire to live their lives in accordance to those very scriptures.

However, before anyone decides to cast both of these groups in the same mold, a few facts need to be stated:

- The *Bible* does not teach or otherwise promote conquest or persecution of those who are in disagreement or opposition to its precepts.
- Those who in years past called themselves "Christian" and claimed the *Bible* as justification for conquest or persecution were not true Christians and received the motivation to conquer from sources other than the *Bible.*
- The Koran, on the other hand, succinctly dictates conquest, persecution, and even the murder of "infidels" who will not convert to the Islamic faith.
- While Christian Fundamentalists may use terms like "militant" or "soldiers of Christ" to describe themselves, these are not in the context of persecution or conquest. The militant Christian Fundamentalist uses this verbiage in the context of waging an intellectual and spiritual war of words and lifestyle in "Defense of the Faith" against those who oppose the truth of the Word of God.

> This war is *always* to be conducted in the spirit of love toward the opposition while never condoning or supporting any position that is opposed to the teachings of the Word of God.

Some may argue that the Crusades and the Inquisition contradict this position of fundamental Christianity, but one must remember that both of these campaigns were ordered and executed by the Roman Catholic Institution—by no means true Christianity--much less fundamentalist in any respect of the term. During the Crusades and the Inquisition, any who opposed the Church of Rome: Moors, Jews, true Christians, and Gnostics, all faced the same possible fate—extermination at the hands of the Pope. The Crusades were not "holy warfare;" but rather, these campaigns were quests motivated by greed and the lust for power--hardly biblical objectives.

Therefore, to label all who call themselves "fundamentalists" in various religions as an alliance of evil forces is completely unfounded. Yet the new paradigm evangelicals have a distinct tendency to do just that. As a matter of fact, Dr. Rick Warren has made his position on Christian Fundamentalism very clear. In 2005 he stated:

> "Today there really aren't that many Fundamentalists left. I don't know if you know that or not, but they are such a minority; there aren't that many Fundamentalists left in America...Now the word Fundamentalist actually comes from a document in the 1920s called the *Five Fundamentals of the Faith.* And it is a very legalistic, narrow view of Christianity." (3)

It is true that the term "Fundamentalist" did originate in 1920 with a declaration of *The Five Fundamentals*. However, in spite of Dr. Warren's condescending opinion, these "Five Fundamentals" were not set forth as a narrow view of Christianity; but rather as a definitive defense of true Christianity as opposed to the rise of what is now termed as Modernism. Modernism is a philosophy within the organized "church" that denies the Virgin Birth of Christ, the Deity of Christ, His Vicarious Blood Atonement, His Bodily Resurrection, and other cardinal doctrines of the Scripture. Those who were deemed as Fundamentalist in the 1920s were those men and women who remained true to the Word of God in opposition to those who chose to erase those passages that taught these vital doctrines.

Half a century after the publication of *The Five Fundamentals*, the detailed definition of a "Fundamentalist" was explicitly presented by the World Congress of Fundamentalists:

> *"A Fundamentalist is a born-again believer in the Lord Jesus Christ who*
>
> 1) Maintains an immovable allegiance to the inerrant, infallible, and verbally Inspired Bible;
> 2) Believes whatever the Bible says is so;
> 3) Judges all things by the Bible, and is judged only by the Bible;
> 4) Affirms the foundational truths of the historic Christian Faith:
>   a. The doctrine of the Trinity
>   b. The incarnation, virgin birth, substitutionary atonement, bodily resurrection, ascension into Heaven, and Second Coming of the Lord Jesus Christ
>   c. The new birth through regeneration of the Holy Spirit
>   d. The resurrection of saints to life eternal
>   e. The resurrection of the ungodly to final judgment and eternal death
>   f. The fellowship of the saints, who are the body of Christ;
> 5) Practices fidelity to that faith, and endeavors to preach it to every creature;
> 6) Exposes and separates from all ecclesiastical denial of that Faith, compromise with error, and apostasy from the Truth; and
> 7) Earnestly contends for the Faith once delivered.
>
> Therefore, Fundamentalism is a militant orthodoxy with a soul-winning zeal. While Fundamentalists may differ on certain *interpretations* of Scripture, we join in unity of heart and common purpose for the

> defense of the Faith and the preaching of the Gospel, without compromise or division.
>
> Unless a man holds and defends the Faith of Scripture, and is concerned for the salvation of the lost, he is not a true Fundamentalist." (4)

Frankly, by his reference to the *Five Fundamentals* as "legalistic and narrow," Dr. Warren is in reality confirming the Word of God when it states, "narrow is the way that leadeth to life eternal." As for his accusation of "legalistic," what exactly does he mean by that? There are no new laws, rules, or regulations stated in the 1920 document, just as there is no dictate of cultural lifestyle in the 1976 document. Both are doctrinal statements and a commitment of allegiance to those doctrines. Therefore, Dr. Warren's claim that *The Five Fundamentals* are " a very legalistic, narrow interpretation of Christianity" is a virtual endorsement of Modernism---the broad brush version of apostate protestant "Christianity" that has condemned millions to eternal damnation.

FUNDAMENTALISM AND FEAR

The truth of the matter is that it is *doctrine* that causes the most heartburn for men like Dr. Warren, and if he had his way Fundamentalism would disappear from the face of the earth. For postmodern man abhors doctrine, and Dr. Warren believes that any Christian standing on the fundamental doctrines of the Word of God has the potential to alienate multitudes along with their money from the organized church. Therefore, he continues the attack launched by his New Evangelical predecessors in 1948. As reported by Paul Nussbaum in the *Philadelphia Inquirer*:

> "Warren predicts that fundamentalism, of all varieties, will be 'one of the big enemies of the 21st century...Muslim fundamentalism, Christian fundamentalism, Jewish fundamentalism, secular fundamentalism - they're all motivated by fear. Fear of each other.'" (5)

This is one of the most ridiculous statements that Dr. Warren has ever made. Where in the world could he have come up with the idea that

Fundamentalism is driven by fear? Perhaps Dr. Warren agrees with the occult writers of the book, *Spiritual Politics*. This book is "Volume II" of the "New Age Bible," ("Volume I" is *The Aquarian Conspiracy*.) and its authors boldly proclaim:

> "This false sense of separateness is the root of all of our fears." (6)

In light of the discussion of previous chapters, this statement is not only very relevant to the primary theme of this manuscript but also carries with it a deep sense of profundity. For a careful consideration of the primary basis of Christian Fundamentalism reveals "ecclesiastical separation from those who embrace error" as its very cornerstone. However, the occult world, as well as those who ascribe to New Paradigm thought of "third way" philosophies abhor separation. For separation is in diametric opposition to third way group-think philosophy.

Remember Rick Warren's statement, *"The answer to fear is community?"* Consider again the occult philosophy as quoted in Spiritual Politics:

> "An important foundation of the new political transformational paradigm is a spirit of community...The Ageless Wisdom teaches that cooperation is the innate attitude of the soul---it is naturally group conscious rather than individually self-centered." (7)

So here is illustrated directly "from the horse's mouth" the occult contention that one is to fear separation and embrace a sense of "community." However, the Bible is very clear in its contention of ecclesiastical separation from those who deny the fundamental doctrines of the faith. Furthermore the Bible is also very clear that false teachers are to be exposed and expelled from the local church. The Apostle Paul, under the direction of the Holy Spirit, did not mince words when he stated:

> "What concord hath Christ with Belial? Or what part hath he that believeth with an infidel? And what agreement hath the temple of God with idols? ...Wherefore, come

> out from among them and be ye separate, and touch not the unclean thing."(8)

Thus, in spite of what Dr. Warren may say or think, Christian Fundamentalism and its ecclesiastical separation is not motivated by fear of other forms of fundamentalism. As a matter of fact, the only fear that inspires Christian Fundamentalism is the biblical fear of a Holy God. The Fundamentalist Christian follows the direction of Jesus Himself when He proclaimed:

> "...Be not afraid of them that kill the body and after that have no more that they can do. But I will forewarn you whom ye shall fear. *Fear Him, which after He hath killed hath the power to cast into hell; yea, I say unto you, fear Him.*" (9)

If this command of Jesus is followed, the true Christian Fundamentalist is not only unmotivated by fear of other forms of religious fundamentalism, but the true believer is strongly motivated to just the opposite -- courage. This courage is not the mere mortal courage of the brave, but spiritually imparted courage to stand in the face of any opposition --for the Christian Fundamentalist stands courageously and unapologetically on the truth of the Word of God.

Therefore, it is the contention of this author that it is *Dr. Warren and his accomplices who are* motivated by fear---*fear of the doctrinal truth taught by the Word of God.* For if Rick Warren, Bill Hybels, Leith Anderson, John Maxwell, Dan Southerland, Bob Buford, Ted Haggard, Ken Blanchard, or any of the other New Paradigm Evangelicals would take a firm stand on the fundamental doctrines of the Word of God, their postmodern constituents would abandon them faster than the proverbial speeding bullet of *Superman* fame.

Additionally, anyone who follows the New Paradigm model most certainly personifies the Scripture that states. "there is no fear of God before their eyes." (10) For any individual who would dare to lower Jesus Christ to a human level at every possible opportunity, institute human business practices to advance spiritual initiatives, utilize psychology as biblical principle, train "Christian" leaders with secular behavioral sciences, base their "Christianity" on the principles of Gnosticism, and/or use the terminology and teachings of witchcraft and the occult world to promote church growth has absolutely no fear of the holy, transcendent, and Almighty God described in this author's *Bible.*

Based on all of the above, could Dr. Warren's statements on Fundamentalism be just another coincidence? Is his rabid opposition to Fundamentalism in reality the manifestation of deeper doctrinal issues? If the doctrinal issues are indeed the problem, which doctrines are creating such conflict as to be so offensive to New Paradigm Evangelicals? Finally, and most importantly, which doctrines listed in the *Five Fundamentals* or by the 1976 World Congress of Fundamentalism could one reject and still be truly born again?

NEW PARADIGM CHURCH OR ONE WORLD RELIGION ?

Only God knows the heart, and only God knows the future. However, the born-again child of God must rest on the principles of the written Word of God and not on the humanistic methods of men. The issues discussed in this chapter expose serious error in the new paradigm philosophy that leads one to conclude that the Purpose Driven, Church Growth Movement is indeed a new false Christianity engendering a new generation of professing Christianity that denies and negates the doctrinal teachings of Scripture. Such a pseudo-faith most assuredly personifies the Laodicean church of *Revelation* Chapter 3.

One can only speculate as to the end of this matter. However, just as Modernism created the antithesis of the dialectical equation, "third way" new paradigm thought is truly the *synthesis*--the religion of the new radical center. Any religion that is so willing to embrace the occult group-think philosophy is certainly a candidate for the centrist "neither hot nor cold" Church of Laodicea that will be spewed out of the mouth of God and into the awaiting arms of Antichrist.

To make matters worse, in 2005 leading evangelicals and Roman Catholics yoked themselves together with yet another mutual document. Since the initial *Evangelicals and Catholics Together* statement 10 years ago, there have been six such documents in which evangelical leaders took a position of compromise and joined the Vatican in the "culture war." According to *The Berean Call:*

> "It comes at a time when conservative protestants and Roman Catholics have overcome theological differences in an effort to work together on causes of mutual concern, such as opposition to same-sex marriages and assisted suicide." (11)

Signers of this agreement include Chuck Colson, Timothy George, the disgraced Ted Haggard, and of course, Dr. Rick Warren. The fact is that more cooperation with Catholicism continues to erode what little doctrinal position the Church of the New Paradigm has left. So now, not only are occult philosophies permeating this group, but continuing cooperation with Catholicism enhances the possibilities of an emerging one world Laodicean religion.

Are Rick Warren, Bob Buford, Bill Hybels, and the others truly creating the "end of the age" pseudo–Christianity of Laodicea? Of that we cannot be absolutely certain, but there are realities embedded within this scenario of which one can be absolutely dogmatic:

- The one world religion of Antichrist will absolutely come to pass.
- The syncretism of occult group-think philosophy with moderate Christianity negates and perverts the Gospel of Grace.
- The allegiance to and adoption of the methods of Drucker, Senge and other globalist social planners is laying the groundwork for a one world religion.
- As will be seen in the next chapter, the P.E.A.C.E. program will open dangerous ecumenical dialogue with religious individuals who are not only positioned in opposition to true Christianity, but who are also sworn to annihilate it.

These and other realities must be constant reminders that the Purpose-Driven, Seeker-Sensitive Church of the New Paradigm is not building the Kingdom of God, but rather, *Rebuilding the Tower of Babel* that will result in the One World Church.

END NOTES

(1) Warren, Rick. *Learn to Love Yourself,* Ladies Home Journal, March, 2005.

(2) II Corinthians 12:9.

(3) Warren. Speech to the Pew Forum on Religion, May 23, 2005.

(4) Beale, David O. *In Pursuit of Purity: American Fundamentalism Since 1850*, Unusual Publications, Greenville, SC, 1986. p.348

(5) Nussbaum, Paul. *The Purpose-driven Pastor*, The Philadelphia Inquirer, Sunday, January 8, 2006, http://www.philly.com/mld/inquirer/living/religion/13573441.htm

(6) McLaughlin, Corrie and Davidson, Gordon. *Spiritual Politics*, Ballantine Books, New York, 1994, p. 148.

(7) Ibid. p.121.

(8) II Corinthians 6:15-17.

(9) Luke 12:4-5.

(10) Romans 3:18.

(11) *The Berean Call* Newsletter. www.updates@tbc.org. January 2, 2007.

Chapter 7

Where There is Smoke...

"If it looks like a duck, walks like a duck, and quacks like a duck; we can be reasonably assured that it is a small aquatic creature of the family Anatidae." (1)

In the late 19th Century, the British Empire spanned the entire globe, and the Union Jack was firmly planted on every continent on the face of the earth. This most benevolent and sophisticated of world empires never saw the sun set on its vast territorial frontier, and it was from the United Kingdom that the Word of God was disseminated to the foremost regions of the earth. However, with the Victorian era came a biblical eschatology that had its conception more in the gilded halls of the Vatican than in the sacred pages of the Word of God --- *Postmillennial Dominion Theology*.

Postmillennial Dominion Theology teaches that the Church is the manifested Kingdom of God on Earth, and that this kingdom will grow to the point of producing a theocratic world government prior to and in anticipation of the Return of Christ. Even many of those in the 19th Century whose theology was otherwise completely fundamental were snared in the net of "pigeon-holing" their own current events into an eschatology that apparently revealed that the Kingdom of God on Earth was to be fully manifested in the vast British Empire.

By the middle of the 19th Century, a generation of men arose that were determined to extend the United Kingdom to over the entire earth. These men were led by wealthy individuals like Cecil Rhodes and Lord Alfred Milner. Rhodes, Milner, and their followers were determined to build a new world order from the baseline of Great Britain that would bring to fruition the long awaited Kingdom of God on Earth. The 20th Century descendants of the Rhodes legacy founded the Institute of International Affairs in Great Britain along with their U.S counterparts who formed the Council on Foreign Relations.

Most relevant to the discussion of this manuscript, men of the Rhodes legacy like Lionel Curtis fervently held to a one-world philosophy that echoed the values of the *Golden Rule* and the *Sermon on the Mount.* Because of the religious nature and bent of these world federalists of the early 20th Century, it comes as no surprise that they saw the established church as the catalyst to achieve a world government. As a matter of fact, Curtis himself asserted that "the church alone can create the necessary public opinion for the establishment of the commonwealth of God." (2)

However, there was a problem. How does a political entity grow from a spiritual philosophy? The answer was easily discovered – recruit the clergy to mix a political message with the spiritual. The implementation of this concept turned out to be a rousing success in the United States. John Foster Dulles, who shared with Curtis the concept that the ethical teachings of Christ were the most dynamic force in history, was the perfect man for the job. It was then Dulles who became the perfect liaison between the Council on Foreign Relations and the modernist clergy of the Federal Council of Churches. (3)

At this point, one must understand the basis of the Curtis/Dulles philosophy. The idea that the "ethical teachings of Jesus" are the most dynamic in history is absolutely true. However, to place all of the emphasis on Christ's "ethical teaching" while ignoring His doctrine opens the floodgates to a "social gospel" as the primary mission and focus of the church. This is exactly what happened in the early 20th Century. The active participation of Dulles in the Federal Council of Churches resulted in the widespread dissemination of a political/religious/social philosophy. As relayed by Martin Erdmann in *Building the Kingdom of God*:

> "While the church still frequently mentioned the problem of sin, it was usually in the context of sin against society rather than sin against God. Regeneration was masterfully redefined as a new social awareness. The substitutionary atonement of Christ upon the cross was deemed insignificant and was rarely if ever mentioned... that humankind can find peace with God only by being justified by faith, was simply ignored as without relevance." (4)

The end result was an apostate professing church whose leaders became the stooges of the globalist elite of Institute of International Affairs and the Council on Foreign Relations. Instead of preaching the Gospel of Grace, these modernist ministers unwittingly promoted the internationalist agenda of the architects of a world government and a world religion.

HISTORY DOES INDEED REPEAT ITSELF

The followers of Rhodes, Milner, and their disciples wrote a script to build a new society. They envisioned a world with a society based on the values that emerged for the ethical teachings of Jesus without His doctrine. This was exactly as noted by Marilyn Ferguson in *The Aquarian Conspiracy*:

> *"The radical center of spiritual experience seems to be knowing without doctrine."* (5)

In fairness, Marilyn Ferguson penned these words as an observation--not a prediction of the activities described thus far in this chapter. In essence, occultic writer Marilyn Ferguson confirmed that the spirituality of Rhodes, Curtis, and Dulles is indeed not true Christian spirituality. Quite to the contrary, this spirituality can be biblically described as the working of the "Spirit of Antichrist."

The most relevant observation in the context of this manuscript, however, is not historical---but contemporary. For the obvious bridge between the between the CFR, John Foster Dulles, and the Federal Council of Churches and to their even yet unrealized *Commonwealth of God* is the relationship between the Peter Drucker, New Evangelicals led by Dr. Rick Warren, and the Council on Foreign Relations.

DRUCKER AND WARREN

As has been noted earlier in this manuscript, Peter Drucker was not only a management guru for big business but also served in the same capacity for conservative evangelicals. The Peter Drucker Foundation was organized by Texas evangelical, Bob Buford, and Drucker along with

Buford worked with the large evangelical churches of 1000 members or more to catapult these churches into a rapid growth mode. During this process, Drucker developed a very close relationship with Dr. Rick Warren of Saddleback Community Church south of Los Angeles.

Drucker was a globalist. He envisioned the infamous "3-legged stool" model to develop a spirit of "community " among all mankind. (6) The third "leg" of this stool was the "non-profit sector" that included churches. This sector, however, posed to be a major obstacle for Drucker's model. For fundamentalist and conservative evangelical Christians were not cooperating in the efforts to build this "new society" of peace and love between all of mankind. Therefore, Drucker sought a champion to be groomed to lead a vast volunteer army of nominal Christians to achieve the elusive spirit of community.

Dr. Rick Warren, on the other hand, is technically a Baptist minister. Saddleback Community Church is a member of the Southern Baptist Convention even though the designation of "Baptist" is intentionally omitted from its name. Rick Warren is also a card-carrying New Evangelical and a graduate of the bastion of the "evangelical left," Fuller Theological Seminary. With his recent P.E.A.C.E. plan, he has proven that he is the classic New Evangelical in the spirit of Dr. Harold Ockenga. As noted in a previous chapter, it was Ockenga who determined to reform Fundamentalism by addressing the social issues that fundamentalists avoided and including with salvation a "social philosophy." In addition to Ockenga's social philosophy, Dr. Warren's *purpose-driven* pedagogy embraced Marilyn Ferguson's concept of "knowing without doctrine."

Thus, Drucker, Warren, Buford and their followers fell right in step to initiate "Phase II" of the plan of Dulles and the Federal Council of Churches. Drucker was without doubt an "elitist social planner" as was Dulles, and Warren is an opportunistic religious zealot that is willing to do "whatever it takes" to grow his church, promote his P.E.A.C.E. plan, and advance the new evangelical philosophy of Harold Ockenga regardless of the teachings and commandments of the Word of God.

Realistically, the Drucker/Warren relationship is an evolution of deception. For the apostasy of mainline protestant denominations who joined first the Federal Council and later the National and World Council of Churches were involved in a direct "frontal attack" that failed miserably. The great Ecumenical Movement of the 1960s that was a result of the efforts of the CFR, Dulles, the Vatican, and the WCCC failed. Throngs of individuals fled the stone-cold protestant denominations that denied the Deity of Christ, His Virgin Birth, His Blood Atonement, and His Bodily Resurrection for the biblically safe haven of Fundamentalism and conservative Evangelicalism. Therefore, the time had come for the implementation of Phase II-- a more subtle, much more deceptive approach to the problem. The new "third way" apostasy would project a conservative image while working to accomplish the globalistic goals of Rhodes, Ruskin, Milner, Curtis, and Dulles.

The Drucker/Warren relationship has been previously detailed in this manuscript and prominently included in the long list of "coincidences" that serve as circumstantial evidence in an indictment against Warren and others involved in the Church of the New Paradigm. However, even in the face of a list that casts a dark cloud of dispersion on the Church Growth Movement, is the dark cloud just a coincidental natural phenomenon---or is it smoke? If it is indeed smoke, where is the fire?

WHERE THERE IS SMOKE.... *THERE IS FIRE*

Many readers of this manuscript may feel that Dr. Rick Warren has been the object of undue criticism. After all, he is attracting multitudes with his books, his message, and his methodology. Still, the questions abound. To exactly what or to whom are these multitudes being drawn? Superficially, it all sounds so good. . .so spiritual ...but yet there is the nagging reality that these programs and methods not only do not align with the Word of God but upon even casual scrutiny are diametrically opposed to the doctrines of Scripture. So then, is this movement actually as Dr. Warren claims, "The beginning of a new spiritual awakening, a global movement, a new Reformation," or is it just the white-washed injection of occult and pagan philosophy into the "Greater Evangelical Community?" The fact of the matter is that the allegations are very serious---doctrinal irregularity, witchcraft, pantheism, mysticism, religious infidelity (apostasy), globalism, radical environmentalism, and occult connections. Are all of these accusations merely a lot of smoke from the hot air of Dr. Warren's accusers? Or is it smoke originating from a truly raging wildfire?

As serious as these accusations may be, the leaders of the CGM and Dr. Warren in particular seem constructed of fire-proof, "Teflon" skin—nothing incriminating sticks. Rick Warren, for example, has persuaded many the most experienced conservative Christian authors and researchers that his position is not only biblically based, but that he deserves their prayers and support of all his programs. In spite of all of his support, the events of the second half of 2005 and 2006 have proven to be such serious violations of a Scriptural posture that Dr. Rick Warren, "America's Pastor," has proven beyond any doubt that his "Kingdom building" activities are in reality nothing more than the construction process of *Rebuilding the Tower of Babel.*

RICK WARREN, A GLOBAL STRATEGIST?

Rick Warren seems to have an issue with pride. He certainly does not come across as the humble servant of Jesus Christ. Actually, he comes across as more of a game show host. To illustraate this tendency, on his own website, www.rickwarren.com, Dr. Warren has apparently become a "legend in his own mind" and labels himself (among other things) as a "Global Strategist:"

> "As a global strategist, Dr. Warren advises leaders in the public, private, and faith sectors on leadership development, poverty, health, education, and faith in culture. He has been invited to speak at the United Nations, the World Economic Forum in Davos, the African Union, the Council on Foreign Relations, Harvard's Kennedy School of Government, TIME's Global Health Summit, and numerous congresses around the world. TIME magazine named him one of "15 World Leaders Who Mattered Most in 2004" and in 2005 one of the "100 Most Influential People in the World." Also, in 2005 U.S. News & World Report named him one of "America's 25 Best Leaders." (7)

While his list of credentials is impressive, pride would eventually lead to one of the most shocking revelations concerning Dr. Warren listed in this entire manuscript. However, before evaluating the "smoking gun," there are other events over that last 2 years that build a very incriminating case against the man and his true motives.

As one looks back on the years of 2005 and 2006, his or her thoughts will more than likely focus on the political unrest resulting from the war in Iraq, the Republicans loss of control of the House of Representatives as well as the Senate, the popularity of President Bush II plummeting into free-fall, and the execution of Saddam Hussein. On the religious front, the mainline Protestant denominations continued to move closer to the Vatican, scandal hit the National Association of Evangelicals with the fall of Ted Haggard, the death of Dr. Jerry Falwell, and Dr. Rick Warren put his P.E.A.C.E. plan into high gear.

In the process of promoting his new plan late in 2005, Dr. Warren revealed his true colors. This revelation would wash away all inference of coincidence and transform all previously noted coincidences into hard evidence that goes far beyond coincidence. Thus an examination of just a few of many possible events that will not only bring the picture into perfect focus, but will also reveal the disturbing reality of runaway apostasy within the ranks of the professing Church.

DR. WARREN AT THE ASPEN INSTITUTE

In July of 2005, Dr. Rick Warren appeared as a featured speaker at the Aspen Ideas Festival sponsored by the Aspen Institute of Humanistic Studies. The Aspen Institute, with headquarters in Princeton, NJ and Aspen, Colorado, was founded in 1950 by Walter Paepeke. The AIHS describes itself as an "international non-profit organization dedicated to informed dialogue and inquiry on issues of global concern." (8) According to *Wikipedia*, the on-line encyclopedia:

> "AIHS seeks to bring together leading citizens from private and public sectors of the U. S. and abroad to consider interrelated issues of the human mind and spirit in contemporary society. The group believes that immersion in the Humanist tradition can make

> participants in its program better decision makers. The Institute holds seminars primarily for business executives 'for reflection, rediscovery of personal values, and examination of contemporary issues in the company of some of the best minds in the world' and gives cross-cultural training 'to go beyond immediate business issues to the underlying questions faced in all cultures.'" (9)

This definition is highly enlightening when one realizes that to study the issues of the human mind and spirit by the standard of the "humanist tradition" is nothing more than "spiritual humanism" as illustrated by occult or "new age" thought. In way of clarification, the "Humanist Tradition" is the path of H. G. Wells and the Fabian Socialists who sought to elevate human beings to the status of God. Taking this philosophy to its logical conclusions, one is led to Theosophy and the teachings of Blavatsky, Bailey, and Ferguson.

Therefore, the Aspen Institute is nothing more than the organized mind trust of the philosophies of Blavatsky, H. G. Wells, Aldous Huxley, Alice Bailey, Marilyn Ferguson, and the others already mentioned in this manuscript. To make matters worse, the Aspen Institute interjects the monetary and political aspects of these philosophies into its curriculum to produce an elitist, globalist think tank. To that end, its membership roles include such noted globalist elites as Henry Kissinger, Richard Gardner, Paul Volker, and Robert McNamara. (10)

Another notable member of the Aspen Institute of Humanistic Studies is Harlan Cleveland. From 1974 to 1980 Cleveland developed and directed the Program in International Affairs of the Aspen Institute. Cleveland is a former Assistant Secretary of State and Ambassador to NATO under Lyndon Johnson. He is also a member of the CFR, Club of Rome, and a Rhodes Scholar. As noted by Peter LaLonde in his book, *One World Under the Antichrist*:

> "He originally codified the concept of *piecemeal functionalism*. He observed that trying to directly create a New World Order through organizations such as the U.N. had not worked. By employing the concept of

piecemeal functionalism, these groups expect to achieve broader success. By appearing to address separate issues piece by piece, treaty by treaty, law by law, issue by issue, and organization by organization, the New World Order is being assembled and the religion of the radial center is one virtually unnoticed." (11)

Primarily due to the work of men like Cleveland and fellow Aspen member Richard Gardner, the concept of piecemeal functionalism has become the very foundation of the wildly successful "third way" politics and religion. In this case, the process of disguising a radical religious agenda under the cloak of conservative values or even fundamental doctrinal statements is the key to this success. The failure of Modernism taught elitist global planners that overt, rabid denial of fundamental doctrinal positions will be met with a mass exodus into the camp of the biblically-based Fundamentalists. Essentially, such actions would result in a replay of the events that transpired from 1955-1970. However, *if fundamental doctrine is predominately displayed but never taught*, the opportunity to tear down those doctrinal beliefs one piece at a time mimics the frog in a pot of water brought to a slow boil. Thus, while overtly claiming to fulfill the "Great Commission," the Church of the New Paradigm, through its purpose-driven methodology is subtly destroying the last vestiges of the true New Testament Church and biblical Christianity.

Once one understands these aspects of the Aspen Institute, there is no longer any mystery as to why Dr. Warren would participate in its Ideas Festival. The Aspen Institute is promoting his own "third way" agenda. As a matter of fact, further enlightenment comes when assessing Dr. Warren statements. While serving as a panelist to discuss *The Problem of Evil*, Dr. Warren said:

"In fact, I don't think evil and sin are the same... We don't know the answers...we really don't...none of us are going to come out at the end of the day and say 'got that one figured out.' If you do please write the book on it and I will buy it.....*I don't think it [evil] is the same thing as sin*...I don't consider myself an evil person because I sin...I think you have to reserve the word 'evil' for

> 'evil'....I haven't yet found a good definition of it...maybe Peter has. I was the one who suggested this topic by the way because I wanted to hear what Alan and Peter had to say about it because these are two men I have respected for years and read all their stuff and I really came to take notes....We can become an evil person by making bad choices....I think evil is metastization where it just takes over...." (12)

Based on previous discussions, there should be no surprise that Dr. Warren would have an issue with calling sin "evil," or thinking of the sinner as "evil." After all, that would contradict everything he wrote in the *Ladies Home Journal* article discussed in the last chapter. Based on Dr. Warren's perspective, how can lost sinners have any self-esteem if they view themselves as evil? If this were the case, one must conclude that mankind has evolved to a higher moral plane since the Apostle Paul penned by inspiration of the Holy Spirit:

> *"Jesus Christ came to save sinners, among whom I am chief."* (13)

Paul cannot be interviewed for confirmation of his intentions with this statement, but based on just the context of the passage one can be perfectly justified in concluding that Paul would have openly confessed that prior to his faith in Jesus Christ, he was in fact "evil." Furthermore, one can be just as certain that Paul would state without equivocation that sin is the personification of "evil." Lastly, Paul would undoubtedly confirm that the "desperately wicked" heart of man and the "old nature" that still lodges within the redeemed are both "evil."

The root of the problem faced by Dr. Warren stems from the fact that when one puts himself into a forum with occultists, globalists, and infidels he must resort to double-talk and semantics to impress his audience while not offending his constituents who will most assuredly be viewing video of the event. Thus he finds himself making biblically absurd statements and praising those who are the enemies of the Gospel of Jesus Christ.

For example, consider Dr. Warren's co-panelist, Rev. Peter Gomes. Rev. Gomes is a professor and Chairman of Christian Morals at the Harvard University. He is also is openly gay (14), and is a universalist - - so much for Christian *and* morals! Yet in spite of all of this, Dr. Warren proclaims that he is a great admirer of Gomes and has read *all* his works.

Dr. Warren's participation at the Aspen Institute and his praise of Dr. Gomes leaves no room whatsoever of coincidence. In the first place, a true conservative Baptist preacher would never receive an invitation to appear on any panel at the Aspen Institute. This "priviledge" is reserved for only the globalist elite. Secondly, anyone who is a true "Defender of the Faith" would never accept an invitation from any "new age" humanist organization. Neither would a man of God praise one who would be best categorized as an "infidel." This instance equates not only to more smoke --- but a roaring fire.

DR. WARREN AT THE UNITED NATIONS

There is absolutely no question that the United Nations was established as the beach head of a world government. This was an open and highly debated topic in the 1950s, and it was obvious that many members of Legislative Branch of the United States Government were flagrantly opposed to not only its existence but also to the participation of the United States as a member of this organization. As the years passed, however, opposition to the U.N. declined to the point that most outcries were limited to far right wing organizations such as the John Birch Society. Along with this decline in opposition came a general apathy toward the organization, and its effectiveness and influence by the time of the Reagan Administration was minimal.

However, with the injection of increased U.S. funding and support during the reign of Bush I and the subsequent "third way" politics of Bill Clinton, the efforts of a decade of *piecemeal functionalism* began to bear fruit. By the late 1990s the power of the United Nations again began to rise. Today, the U.N. seeks to interject its internationalism into the daily lives of every individual on the face of the earth, and continues to pilfer the bank accounts of U.S. citizens in particular. The U.N. is once again a major player in building a New World Order with initiatives that promote a pagan, globalist agenda.

While the United Nations is indeed a mission field that is "ripe unto harvest," any individual who preaches salvation through Jesus Christ alone is not welcome there—much less given an invitation to speak to its delegates. However, Dr. Rick Warren was offered an invitation to speak at the U.N. Interfaith Prayer Breakfast on the morning of September 13th, 2005.

What an opportunity to preach the Gospel of Jesus Christ to this group! However, the published quotations of Dr. Warren's speech strangely never once mention the name of Jesus Christ. Frankly, he may have been given strict instructions not to mention His name, but should that have mattered? What did he say? The following quotation sums up the theme of his discourse:

> "The Bible says God is love. It doesn't say He has love. Love is the essence of His character," he said. "You were created to be loved by God. Being created in God's image, we are to love Him back…I am not here to talk about religion. I am here to talk about a relationship with God." (15)

This statement is typical of the Modernist who denies the blood atonement of Jesus Christ and presents a social gospel of love. Not that what Dr. Warren said was false, but his statements do not tell the whole story as Scripture sums it up:

> "For God so loved the world, that He gave His only begotten Son. That whosoever believeth in Him should not perish but have everlasting life." (16)

The scriptural evidence declares that God's love is personified in the person of Jesus Christ and His sacrifice for the sins of mankind. When one speaks of the "love of God" to an interfaith audience without once mentioning the name of Jesus, then that audience is left to each individual's concept of God, whether that "God" be Allah, Krishna, Buddha, Quetzelcoatl, or Zeus. Thus the heart of the pagan or religious individual who does not know Jesus Christ is in a far worse condition than it was before they heard about the love of this nebulous God.

Additionally, the article that gives the quotations from Dr. Warren's speech states that the effect of those assembled was such that they all immediately joined together in prayer. Now let's get this straight:

- A conservative Southern Baptist preacher speaks to an interfaith gathering at the U.N.

- This preacher fails to name the name of Jesus Christ, but speaks of the love of God.
- All in attendance are compelled to go to God in prayer immediately upon the conclusion of the preacher's speech.

Were then these individuals praying to the true God of the Bible who sacrificed His only begotten Son for the sins of mankind, or were they praying to false gods? Why would a preacher of the Gospel of Jesus Christ seek to lead men to pray to false gods?

The really confusing aspect of this is that this exposition of the "love of God" and a prayer issued to false gods was led by a conservative preacher who declares that the fulfilling of the "Great Commission" as the primary purpose of the Church. On the other hand, if this conservative Southern Baptist preacher was attempting to *Rebuild the Tower of Babel*, would his message be limited to the love of a nebulous God? Would he participate in a prayer in which others in the group were obviously praying to false gods? The answers to these questions lead one to the distinct conclusion that Dr. Warren's presence, presentation, and participation at the United Nations Prayer Breakfast in September of 2005 are far more than coincidental. As a matter of fact, his appearance, speech, and participation at this very event are all aspects of a raging fire producing pluming billows of black smoke.

RICK WARREN AND THE COUNCIL ON FOREIGN RELATIONS

The Council on Foreign Relations is the U.S. "granddaddy" of all the elite globalist organizations on the North American Continent. The CFR was the brainchild of Col. Edward Mandel House, advisor to President Woodrow Wilson. House was instrumental in drafting the Covenant of the League of Nations—the first 20th Century attempt to establish the foundation for a world government. When the U.S. Legislature failed to ratify the League of Nations Charter, he set about to join forces with other disciples of Milner and Rhodes to successfully create the Council on Foreign Relations that became a reality in 1921.

As stated earlier, the CFR was the North American twin to the Royal Institute of International Affairs, and it became the conduit to promote the elitist international agenda. It was through the CFR that globalist agendas were supported and financed via the Rockefeller and Carnegie

Foundations. If there was any doubt as to the organization's intentions, the official seal of the CFR became the image of a man on a white horse---just as the Book of Revelation describes Antichrist in Chapter 6 of that book.

So what possible scenario could connect Dr. Rick Warren to the CFR? The author of this manuscript must now have become certifiably "off his rocker" to make such an association. Really? The story goes like this:

In October of 2006, Dr. Rick Warren went on a road trip. This trip to Europe, the Middle East, and Africa was set up to primarily to promote his P.E.A.C.E. Plan. While he planned to spend the great majority of his time on this trip in Africa, he first stopped in Germany and then in Syria before journeying south to Rwanda. In Syria, he met with President Bashar al-Assad and the Muslim Grand Mufti. This meeting was met with a firestorm of criticism from all corners. The Syrian News Agency released a story indicating that Warren was opposed to the war in Iraq, felt that Syria should be involved in a peace process to resolve the conflict, and other forms of propaganda. Dr. Warren denied all that was reported as untruths, and seemed to weather the storm. Rick Warren further said that his trip to Syria was at the urging of his next door neighbor who is Syrian. He also met with Christian leaders in Syria, reporting that most in the United States have a skewed perception of Syria as a terrorist nation.

Of course all of Dr. Warren's statements, even if 100% true, are nothing more than damage control. Rick Warren's PR department had to work overtime to cover for their boss's miscalculation of the reaction over a trip to Syria to promote his P.E.A.C.E. Plan as consorting with the enemy. In spite of public reaction, there is really no secret here. Warren went to Syria because he probably had an inside contact (maybe it was his neighbor) that could get him in the door to do some serious sales pitches of his global social program to the highest levels of the Syrian government. After all, Islamic nations are a huge untapped market for this sort of thing. Far more significant, however, is the revelation of information resulting from his Syrian holiday that is more like a smoking missile silo than a simple "smoking gun."

The missile from this smoking silo was launched because *WorldnetDaily* editor Joseph Farah was incensed by the actions of Megapastor Rick Warren in Syria. In reading his column, it did not take much imagination to see that Mr. Farah felt that Dr. Warren's actions crossed the line and bordered on high treason. He responded to Warren's trip to Syria with the article *The Purpose-driven Lie* that appeared in *WorldNetDaily* on November 16, 2006. As a result of the appearance of this article, Dr. Warren began to communicate with Joseph Farah by email in order to defend his actions and debunk the "lies" of the Syrian News Agency. This correspondence led to a second article by Farah entitled *Megapastor's Damascus Road Experience* that appeared November 20, 2006.

In all the banter between Warren and Farah in their email conversations as recorded in this article, a shocking revelation exploded into the public eye. The conversation, as recorded by Farah, went as follows:

> "...And lastly I suggested that he (Warren) should have 'counseled with me (Farah), or other people knowledgeable about the Middle East before doing so much damage with your reckless trip...'"
>
> "...He let me know he is a close friend of President Bush 'and many, if not most, of the generals at the Pentagon.'"
>
> "Warren explained that he had also counseled with the National Security Council and the White House, as well as the State Department, before his little courtesy call for a neighbor."
>
> "'In fact,' Warren added, 'as a *member of the Council on Foreign Relations* and Oxford Analytica, I might know as much about the Middle East as you.'" (17)

What did he say? Did Rick Warren just confess that he is a member of the Council on Foreign Relations? The CFR's website reported that Rick Warren was a speaker in its *Religion and Foreign Policy Series* in 2005. This in and of itself signifies "guilt by association" and is at best circumstantially incriminating. However, for Warren to admit that he is a member of this organization cancels all possibility of any coincidence. One does not become a member the CFR by preaching the Gospel. One does not become a member of the CFR for "Defending the Faith." One further does not become a member of the CFR by publicly demanding conformity to the principles of the Word of God.

No, dear friends, one only becomes a member of the CFR by supporting an elitist, globalist agenda to create a Luciferian New World Order. One becomes a member of the CFR to build the "Kingdom of God"described and supported by the Lucis Trust. The same is true for those who speak at the United Nations, the Aspen Institute, and other globalist organizations not mentioned in this manuscript. One only becomes a member of the CFR and a contributor to other globalist organizations to aid in the construction process of *Rebuilding the Tower of Babel.*

END NOTES

(1) Adams, Douglas. *Dirk Gently's Holistic Detective Agency.*
(2) Erdmann, Martin. *Building the Kingdom of God on Earth*, Wipf and Stock Publishers, Eugene, OR. 2005, p.64.
(3) Ibid.
(4) Ibid. p.155.
(5) Ferguson, Marilyn. *The Aquarian Conspiracy*, J.P. Tarcher, Inc., Los Angeles, CA., 1980, P. 377.
(6) For a detailed explanation of the *3-Legged Stool Model* of Peter Drucker, see this author's book, *Outcome-Based Religion*, Chapter 13. This book is available from Cutting Edge Ministries at www.cuttingedge.org.
(7) www.rickwarren.com.
(8) http://en.wikipedia.org/wiki/Aspen_Institute
(9) www.nndb.com/org/760/000051607
(10) LaLonde, Peter. *One World Under Antichrist*, Harvest House Publishers, Eugene, OR, 1991, p.124.
(11) Warren, Rick. As quoted by James Sudquist, *Rick Warren's P.E.A.C.E. Plan vs. Scriptural Teachings on Peace,* http://www.prophecyforum.com/Sundquist/RICKWARREN.htm
(12) I Timothy 1:15.
(13) Sudquist, James. Quoting http://www.creationists.org/resp0013.html, *Rick Warren's P.E.A.C.E. Plan vs. Scriptural Teachings on Peace,* http://www.prophecyforum.com/Sundquist/RICKWARREN.htm

(14) Tse, Rhonda. *Rick Warren Speaks about Purpose at the United Nations,* The Christian Post, Wed., Sept 14, 2005, www.christianpost.com/article/20050914/21340.htm
(15) John 3:16.
(16) Farah, Joseph. *Megapastor Rick Warren's Damascus Road Experience,* www.worldnetdaily.com, November 20, 2006.

Chapter 8

Building the Laodicean Church

Marie B. Hall, wife of noted Masonic author Manly P. Hall, wrote of the hiding place of Francis Bacon's plan to use the American experiment as the manifestation of a New World Order. Mrs. Hall's research revealed among other things, that Francis Bacon and his arcane *Knights of the Helmet* were the guiding force behind the *Constitution of the United States* as well as the *Declaration of Independence.* (1) According to Mrs. Hall and other Baconian experts like Peter Dawkins, these documents were predetermined elements of Bacon's empire-building process.

Interestingly enough, in spite of his Lucerferian philosophies and aspirations, Bacon was also instrumental in the translation of the 1611 King James Version of the Bible. His involvement with the KJV seems quite paradoxical until Marie Hall provides the key to this mystery. For why would a disciple of Lucifer like Bacon have possessed any desire to proliferate the Word of God ? Mrs. Hall explains:

> "A New Constitution for the United Brotherhood of the Earth was built upon enduring principles and anchored at the center of universal law, so that true democracy may be born after its three hundred year prenatal period. *Christianity was recorded, reconciled to scientific law, and correlated to the Secret Doctrine of the East.*" (2)

Here one witnesses first hand the implementation of Luciferic dialectical reasoning:

Thesis +Antithesis= Synthesis.

Christianity was recorded with the translation of the Holy Scriptures and their subsequent availability to the masses. The so-called reconciliation of the Scriptures to "scientific law" occurred when a theology student named Darwin popularized his theories of evolution. Finally, with the rise of the Fabian Socialists, all of the above was correlated to the "Secret Doctrine" which produced what one would now term as *Third Way Spiritual Humanism*. (All of this occurred in Great Britain.)

Thus the formula appears in this fashion:

Christianity (thesis) + The Secret Doctrine (antithesis) = Third Way Spiritual Humanism (synthesis)

One needs but make an honest evaluation of history to see this scenario blatantly displayed across the pages of 19th and 20th Century history. But now, in the 21st Century mankind is witnessing "Phase II" of the implementation of these philosophies. As has been illustrated in this manuscript, the frontal assault on biblical Christianity which began in the early 20th Century suffered a serious setback with the mass exodus from Modernism that resulted in a swelling movement of Fundamentalism. Therefore, something had to be done--- so enter the New Evangelicalism.

The New Evangelical movement that has culminated with Rick Warren's Church of the New Paradigm followed the model of Francis Bacon to the letter:

- The Church of the New Paradigm publicly records Christianity with an evangelical or even fundamental profession and acceptance of the fundamental doctrines of the Word of God.
- The Church of the New Paradigm chooses not to debate matters of science such as the Flood or the age of the earth, thus reconciling Christianity to "scientific law."
- Thanks to the help of men like Peter Drucker, Bob Buford, Ken Blanchard, Bill Hybels, Rick Warren, and many others; occult terminology, concepts of Goddess worship, and principles of witchcraft have been infused into the Church of the New Paradigm. This equates to the Baconian concept of "correlation to the Secret Doctrine." (3)

STOOGES, CONSPIRATORS, OR DUPES

So what of Warren, Buford, Blanchard, Hybels, Anderson, Maxwell, and the other promoters of New Paradigm religious philosophies? The magnitude and gravity of the evidence against them now undoubtedly defies the designation of coincidence. The questions have been asked on previous occasions in this manuscript, but the additional evidence of the last chapter makes the questions worth asking again: Are they conspirators themselves in an unfolding drama to establish a one-world church? Are they simply dupes who have been sold a bill of goods? In fairness, one cannot arbitrarily designate each of those mentioned above in the same category. Even though they obviously share the same philosophy and *modus operandi*, there can be no *indisputable* proof of either guilt or innocence by methodology or association. However, the evidence regarding the leader of this group is very compelling, and the others must in turn be seriously questioned.

As for the *defacto* leader of the movement, Dr. Rick Warren, until the revelation of his CFR membership and the egotistical circumstances under which he revealed this fact; one would have been justifiably compelled to lean toward the "dupe" theory. However, a dupe does not address the U.N. A dupe is not a member of the Council on Foreign Relations, nor is a dupe a member of Oxford Analytica. In order to become a member of either of these organizations, one must already be accepted by the globalist elite and recognized as a one of their own. CFR members in particular are co-conspirators to build a world government and a one world religion. At the very minimum, Dr. Warren had to convince those in authority within the CFR that he was indeed a kindred spirit, and these people are not easily fooled—for they themselves are the masters of subtle deception. The CFR is, in reality and without apology *Rebuilding the Tower of Babel.*

THE BIBLICAL POSITION

So what is the true child of God to do in the face of such a leviathan as the Church of the New Paradigm? What is the biblical position? One needs to consider the following points:

- Separate from any assembly that follows the New Paradigm methodology.
- Warn those involved with New Paradigm assemblies of the deceptive agenda.
- Support a local Fundamental assembly with your attendance, prayers and financial support.

- Pray for your pastor, that he will stand firm in the face of temptation to grow the church by succumbing to the temptations of the purpose-driven, New Paradigm model.
- Be courageous to speak the truth and warn others of the true dangers in study groups that utilize *The Purpose-Driven Life* or other New Paradigm curriculum.
- Determine in your heart to take a stand for the truth—no matter how much you may be criticized by others. (4)

CONCLUSION

Therefore, the true child of God should take to heart the warnings and truths detailed in this manuscript in order to stand against the ancient philosophies of Babel. The born-again individual should look to the example of one who once lived within the shadow of the Tower of Babel--the prophet Daniel. The Book of Daniel records:

> "*Daniel purposed in his heart that he would not defile himself with the portion of the king's meat, nor the wine which he drank...* " (5)

It is very interesting to note that Daniel, in all likelihood had a "ringside view" of the remains of Tower of Babel every day. As a matter of fact:

> "An inscription by Nebuchadnezzar identified the Tower of Borsippa with the Tower of Babel. He restored the base (460 x 690 x 275 ft. high) built 1600 years earlier." (6)

Thus the city of Babylon was built around this monolithic reminder of man's aspirations to build a universal, one-world kingdom. (Of course, Nebuchadnezzar accomplished this very feat with the defeat of Egypt and Pharaoh Necho at the Battle of Carchemesh in 607 BC.) Yet in the face of the success, wealth, glory, notoriety, and power that was at his disposal, Daniel laid his very life on the line in order to be a man that conformed to the principles of Word of God.

What a wonderful example for those of us who live in this present age! Here was a man that witnessed first hand the results of riches and power. Living in the very shadow of the Tower of Babel, he never once recorded that it was a wonderful example of working "in community" (as did Dr. Warren). Furthermore, when facing the personal and direct threat of a world empire and a world religion, he stood firm in his convictions and practices. His devotion to God eventually landed him in the lion's den, but God was faithful to reward His servant for his faithfulness.

So then, will those of us who know the truth be found faithful? Or will we disregard the Scriptures and jump on the New Paradigm Bandwagon? Will we stand for the truth or succumb to criticism? Will we be "salt and light" in a postmodern world or compromise our convictions to follow the crowd?

The roadmap of the future is certain. The Age of Grace will run its course, and Jesus Christ will call the redeemed to the Judgment Seat of Christ and the Marriage Supper of the Lamb. Tragically, for those who remain on the earth after the restraining Holy Spirit is taken away with the Church in the Rapture, the powers of darkness will run roughshod over the entire planet to prepare for the final show-down with the *King of Kings and Lord of Lords.*

In the mean time, the Church is rushing headlong into the age of the "Church of Laodicea" as described in Revelation 3. It is the prophecy of Laodicea that reveals a church just prior to the Rapture that has rejected the truth of the Word of God. It reveals a church that is ostensibly wealthy but does not realize it is spiritually poverty-stricken. It speaks of a church that is much like Jesus' description of the Pharisees---a beautiful whited sepulcher full of dead men's bones. It describes a church full of self-esteem; but yet, a church so misguided in its kingdom-building activities that in lieu of fulfilling its God-ordained mission, it is busy *Rebuilding the Tower of Babel.*

THE END

ENDNOTES

(1) Hall, Marie Bauer. *The Quest for the Bruton Vault*, p. 16.

(2) *Ibid.* p.17.

(3) So as not to confuse the reader, the Baconian plan has been handed many setbacks. In the quest to make America the "New Atlantis," true Christians empowered by the Holy Spirit of God that stood firm on the Word of God permeated the population of the early settlers of North America. It was the efforts of men like Roger Williams and the intervention of Almighty God that made this new nation one that upheld the principles of the Scriptures and overcame the mystical and occultic influence of the masonic philosophies of Bacon and his followers. Further, it was the pioneer spirit of "rugged individualism" that preserved the freedom of the new representative republic and prevented its sliding into a social democracy for more than 200 years.

(4) For a detailed description of the aspects and methods of the Church of the New Paradigm, see the book, *Outcome-Based Religion: Purpose, Apostasy, and the New Paradigm Church* by this author.

(5) Daniel 1:8.

(6) Jeffrey, Grant. *The Signature of God*, Frontier Research Publications, Toronto, Ontario, 1997, pg.40.

ALSO AVAILABLE FROM CUTTING EDGE MINISTRIES

The first book by this author that enables the reader to develop a good grasp of the basics of the New Paradigm Church. (300 pages)

TAPES AND DVDS

Passion, Purpose, &the Paradigm Shift

The whole Christian world is silently going through the dramatic change in religious thinking, called a "Paradigm Shift". Until this shift occurs, Antichrist cannot arise. Once this shift does occur, discerning Christians can know that Antichrist is close. Such a "Paradigm Shift" is now under way, powered by four major factors running together simultaneously. They are: 1) "The Passion of the Christ"; 2) Purpose Driven Church (Rick Warren; 3) "Da Vinci Code" which propagates the Merovingian Bloodline lie, without which Antichrist cannot appear. (VHS, DVD)

Israel, God's Timepiece

As the world trembles on the brink of all-out Regional War, people are asking, "Will Arab – Israeli Conflict Start World War III?" Two full hours of instruction on current events in Israel that will sound like your daily newspaper! This seminar examines the Arab-Israeli conflict, from Old Testament times to our Modern Times. Starts with the God's scattering of the Jews – The Diaspora -- to the founding of Israel in 1948, and finally to the current conflict. The Palestinian issue is thoroughly dealt with, not only in terms of the current struggle, but God's severe plans them. Maps, charts, and pictures makes sense of the places and locations that we hear every day on the news. You will understand that such terms as "Occupied Territories" not only are bogus, but shows the Anti-Semitic nature of the people using this term.This video reveals God's prophetic plan for Israel, prophecy so clear that everyone – including all Arabs – can know the precise outcome of all hostilities. This video will keep you on the edge of your seats as you can just sense the closeness of the end times prophetic hour. (VHS,DVD)

The DaVinci Code: Truth or Myth

Millions of people have read Dan Brown's best seller, *The DaVinci Code*. This book, though a novel, claims to be based on historical facts that not only question, but blatantly attack the deity of Jesus Christ and the divine inspiration of the Holy Scriptures. The simple fact of this matter is that Antichrist cannot arise and successfully claim his lineage back to King David without people believing the Merovingian Blood Line Lie taught by *The DaVinci Code*. This book prepares people for Antichrist! This video is 2 hours long and has 150 colorful PowerPoint slides. (VHS, DVD)

Catholicism, White Sepulcher of Christianity

No one has ever examined the Catholic Church from this unique perspective. You will want all your Roman Catholic loved ones, friends, and co-workers to have this video. You will want all your Liberal, Evangelical Christian friends to see this video also, so they will realize the true nature of the "church" to whom they are moved mightily through Cutting Edge to deliver THE definitive Biblical answer as to why the Catholic Church is producing such a stench from their rotten spiritual fruit. U.S. Format only. (VHS)

NOTES